The Human Body

Other Publications:
WEIGHT WATCHERS® SMART CHOICE RECIPE COLLECTION
TRUE CRIME
THE AMERICAN INDIANS
THE ART OF WOODWORKING
LOST CIVILIZATIONS
ECHOES OF GLORY
THE NEW FACE OF WAR
HOW THINGS WORK
WINGS OF WAR
CREATIVE EVERYDAY COOKING
COLLECTOR'S LIBRARY OF THE UNKNOWN
CLASSICS OF WORLD WAR II
TIME-LIFE LIBRARY OF CURIOUS AND UNUSUAL FACTS
AMERICAN COUNTRY
VOYAGE THROUGH THE UNIVERSE
THE THIRD REICH
THE TIME-LIFE GARDENER'S GUIDE
MYSTERIES OF THE UNKNOWN
TIME FRAME
FIX IT YOURSELF
FITNESS, HEALTH & NUTRITION
SUCCESSFUL PARENTING
HEALTHY HOME COOKING
LIBRARY OF NATIONS
THE ENCHANTED WORLD
THE KODAK LIBRARY OF CREATIVE PHOTOGRAPHY
GREAT MEALS IN MINUTES
THE CIVIL WAR
PLANET EARTH
COLLECTOR'S LIBRARY OF THE CIVIL WAR
THE EPIC OF FLIGHT
THE GOOD COOK
WORLD WAR II
HOME REPAIR AND IMPROVEMENT
THE OLD WEST

This volume is one of a series that examines
various aspects of computer technology
and the role computers play in modern life.

For information on and a full description of
any of the Time-Life Books series listed
above, please call 1-800-621-7026 or write:
Reader Information
Time-Life Customer Service
P.O. Box C-32068
Richmond, Virginia 23261-2068

UNDERSTANDING COMPUTERS

The Human Body

BY THE EDITORS OF TIME-LIFE BOOKS

TIME-LIFE BOOKS, ALEXANDRIA, VIRGINIA

Contents

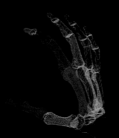

Digital Visions
from Medicine's
Frontiers

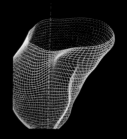

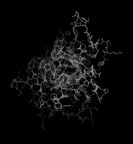

Physicians have always relied to some extent on visual information to help them understand the workings of the human body and intervene when things go wrong. Where their own senses cannot penetrate, science has provided increasingly sophisticated means of making the unseen apparent, from the first ghostly x-rays of the early twentieth century to. today's detail-rich images, which not only show the whole array of tissues, bone, and vessels within the body but can even represent the intricate shapes and structures of molecules. In recent years, the computer has proved itself the key instrument of progress in medical imaging, bringing its information-handling and graphics abilities to bear in many different ways.

Regardless of the application, the computer's contribution is generally twofold. Many of the most sophisticated image-collecting technologies, from x-ray crystallography to magnetic resonance imaging, would not exist without computers, which record, store, and interpret prodigious masses of data. Displaying this data as shapes and colors then becomes the chore of graphics software—specialized programs that translate numbers and mathematical representations into three-dimensional images that can be rotated or even turned into animated sequences. Although many systems aim at realism, symbolic representations more often than not provide the clearest and most informative view.

Perhaps the most revolutionary developments have come from so-called interactive systems, which allow researchers and specialists to manipulate images and thereby simulate procedures or experiments in the harmless environs of computer keyboard and screen. Powerful and speedy processors adjust images almost instantaneously in response to data fed in by the computer's mathematical models of the objects being portrayed. Results are immediately available for visual inspection and analysis.

The following pages only hint at the wide variety of medical applications that are being served by the latest in computer-imaging techniques.

Computerized Portrait of a Key DNA Site

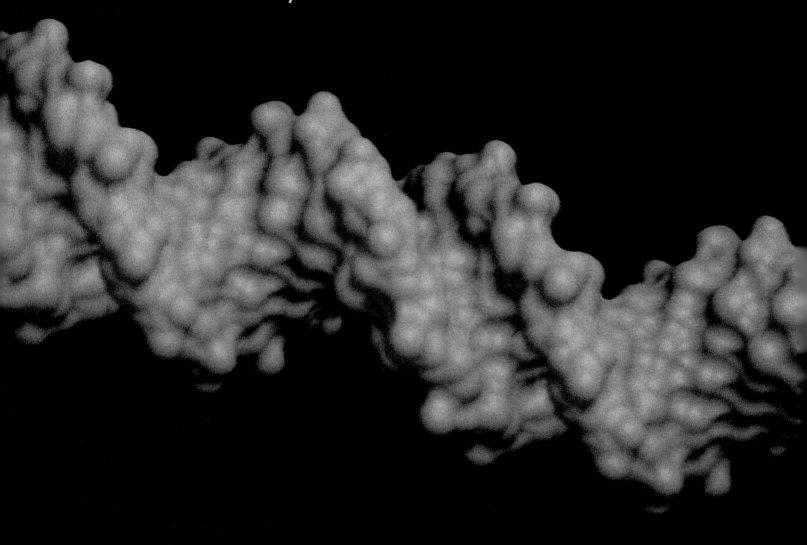

False colors in this computer-generated image give researchers a clear view of the interactions of selected features at an important location along the DNA molecule of a virus. The data on which such images are based is collected by bombarding a crystallized sample with x-rays and recording how the rays are scattered by the crystal's atoms; using complex formulas, a computer analyzes the scatter pattern to determine the sample's molecular structure. Graphics software translates the data into images, here rendering the DNA's surface as a bumpy, hollow shell, purple on the outside and blue on the inside. The cutaway reveals a pair of twisting cords (red) that stand for the sugar-phosphate backbones of the DNA's twin strands. The green and yellow filaments represent the two constituents of a single protein known as a repressor. By binding to this specific segment of the DNA, the repressor in effect turns off the gene responsible for controlling the activity of the virus's other genes. Studying such control mechanisms in simple viral organisms helps researchers gain insights into the more complex workings of human genetic machinery.

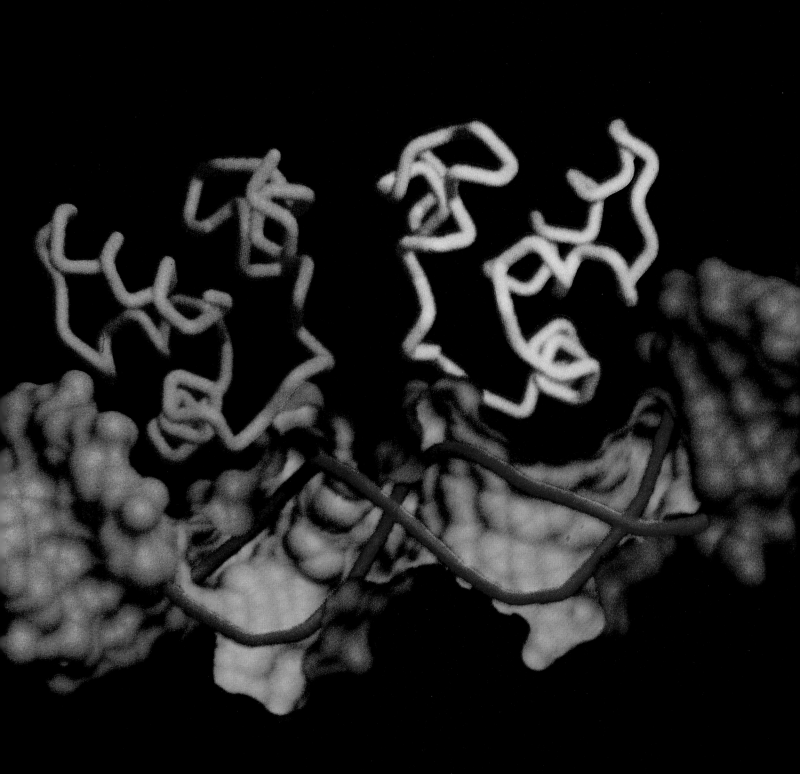

Designing a Drug to Fit an Intricate Web

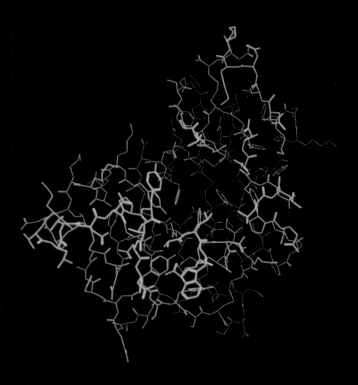

Proteins—the complex chemical compounds that determine how cells function—operate by interacting with other agents in ways that depend on their respective molecular structures. As with DNA, computer-graphics representations of these structures provide an effective means of studying the processes involved. In the images on these pages, white sticks represent the chemical bonds between atoms of an enzyme—a type of protein—that controls the natural inflammation response to injury. At left, to enhance the three-dimensionality of the image, the computer makes foreground sections bright and progressively fades background portions. Clusters of dots *(below, left)* denoting the surface around certain atoms help indicate a pocket within the enzyme's structure. The enzyme will remain inactive until a smaller molecule known as a substrate *(below, yellow)* fits into the pocket as a key fits into a lock, thereby setting in motion the bio-chemical reactions that produce inflammation. Using the computer's graphics to test their results, researchers can experiment with different drug designs intended to short-circuit this inflammation process. A successful drug is one whose molecular structure will bind to the pocket so as to block the substrate *(right)*.

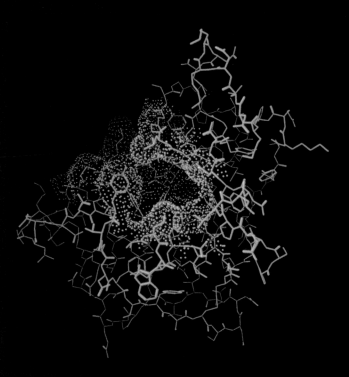

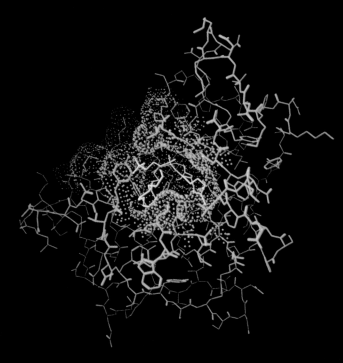

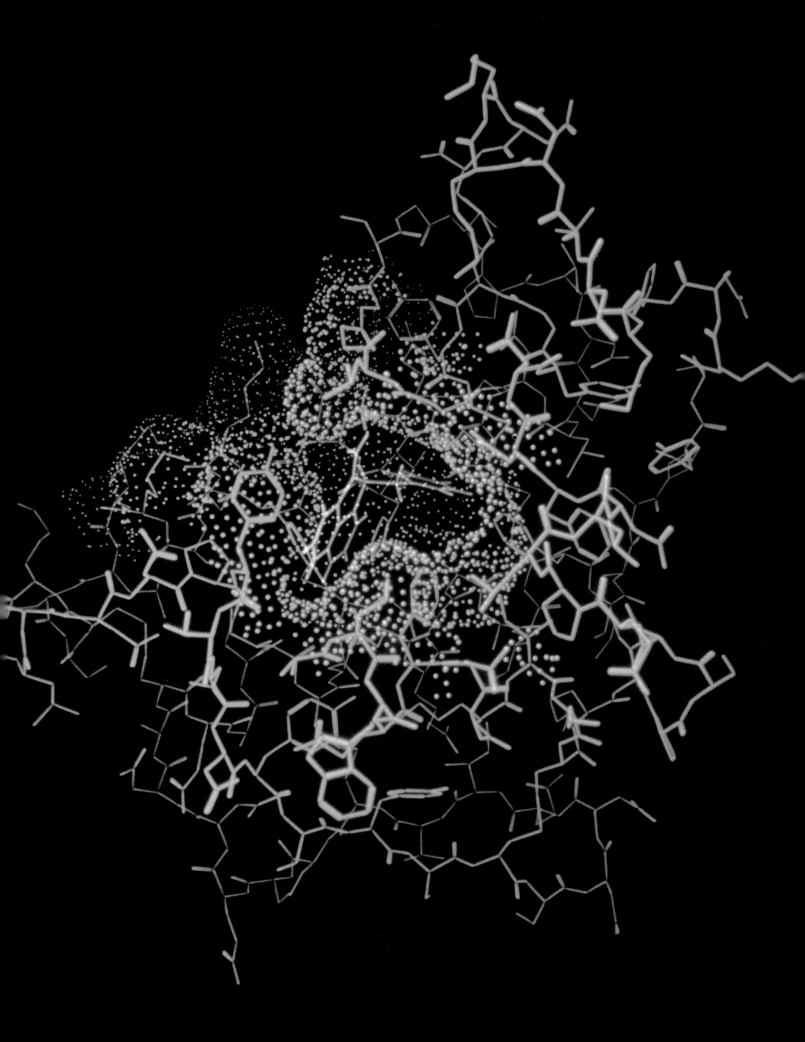

Geometry of a
Heartbeat

This on-screen, three-dimensional
reconstruction of the left ventricle—
the main pumping chamber—of a beat-
ing human heart is the product of combining
computer techniques with one of medicine's most sophisticated image-collecting
technologies, ultrafast computed tomography
(CT). The computer combines information

12

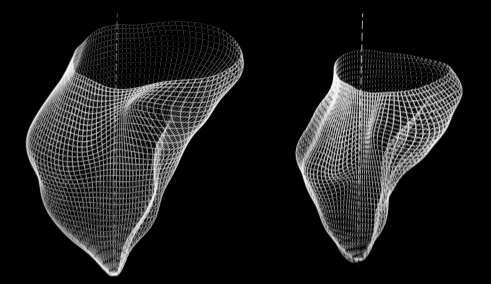

The images at left depict the inner surface of the left ventricle at two critical moments—when it is relaxed *(far left)* and when it is fully contracted. Animated versions combine sequences of these images, each capturing with stop-action clarity a split second during a beat. The wire-frame grid gives the most precise view of the chamber's changing contours, allowing cardiologists to visually assess such factors as the extent of contraction and other aspects of the heart's geometry. Because the images also exist mathematically within the computer, abnormalities can sometimes be identified automatically through calculations or numerical comparisons.

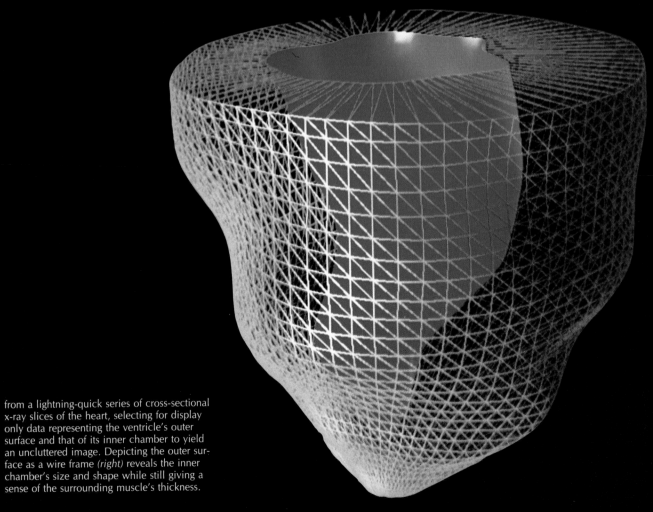

from a lightning-quick series of cross-sectional x-ray slices of the heart, selecting for display only data representing the ventricle's outer surface and that of its inner chamber to yield an uncluttered image. Depicting the outer surface as a wire frame *(right)* reveals the inner chamber's size and shape while still giving a sense of the surrounding muscle's thickness.

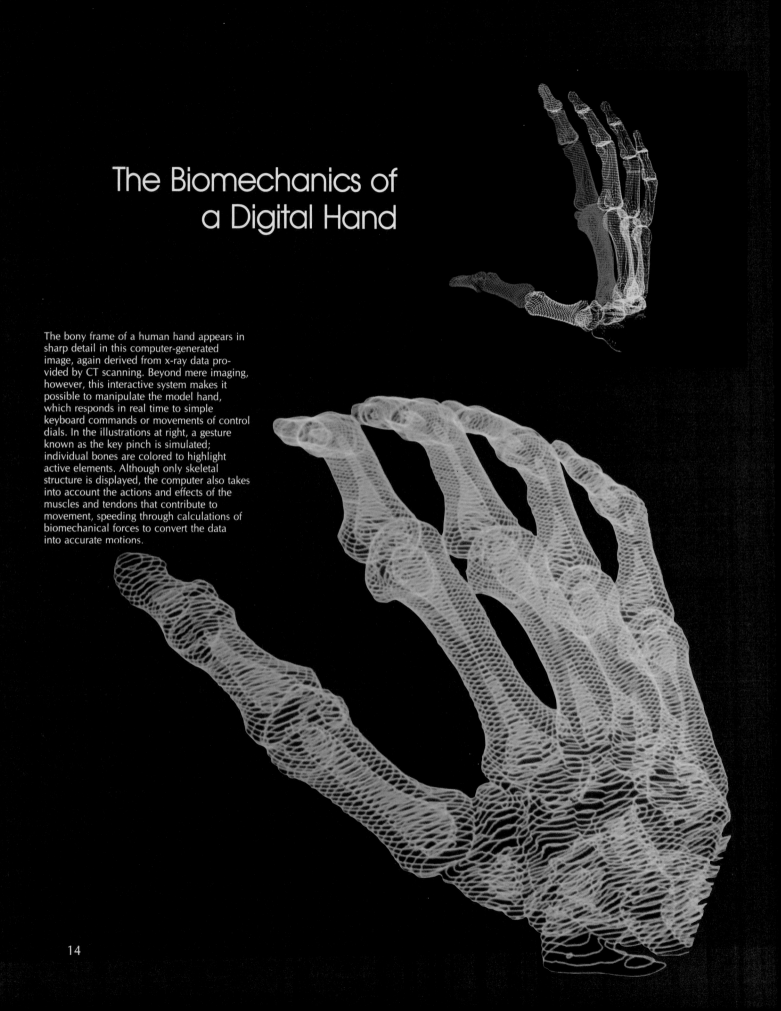

The Biomechanics of a Digital Hand

The bony frame of a human hand appears in sharp detail in this computer-generated image, again derived from x-ray data provided by CT scanning. Beyond mere imaging, however, this interactive system makes it possible to manipulate the model hand, which responds in real time to simple keyboard commands or movements of control dials. In the illustrations at right, a gesture known as the key pinch is simulated; individual bones are colored to highlight active elements. Although only skeletal structure is displayed, the computer also takes into account the actions and effects of the muscles and tendons that contribute to movement, speeding through calculations of biomechanical forces to convert the data into accurate motions.

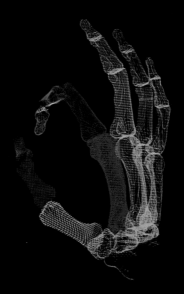

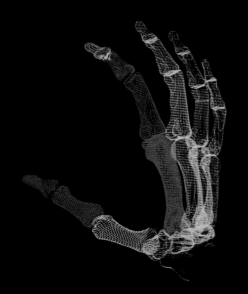

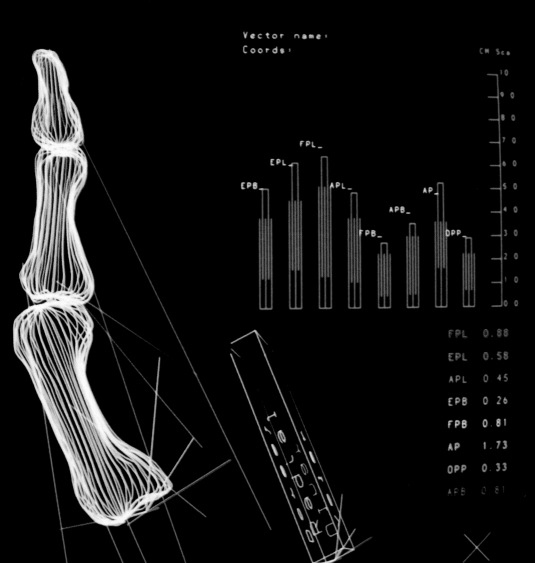

Vector name:
Coords:

CM Sca

FPL_

EPL_

EPB_

APL_

AP_

APB_

FPB_

OPP_

FPL	0.88
EPL	0.58
APL	0 45
EPB	0 26
FPB	0.81
AP	1.73
OPP	0.33
AFB	0 81

An isolation of the thumb indicates the level of detail and degree of interaction available through the computer's graphic displays. The eight muscle-tendon units that move the thumb are represented by the bars at right, which stretch and contract during simulated movements as the actual muscles would. Red lines on the skeletal image correspond to these muscles and show where tendons attach to the thumb bones; the colored numbers to the right are a measurement of each muscle's mechanical ability for the position displayed. The rectangular labeled box orients the view, indicating that this is a left thumb with its back facing to the left. Interactive programming makes it possible to alter these figures to simulate a muscle impairment, say, or to allow a hand specialist to evaluate the mechanical results of a surgical procedure before entering the operating room.

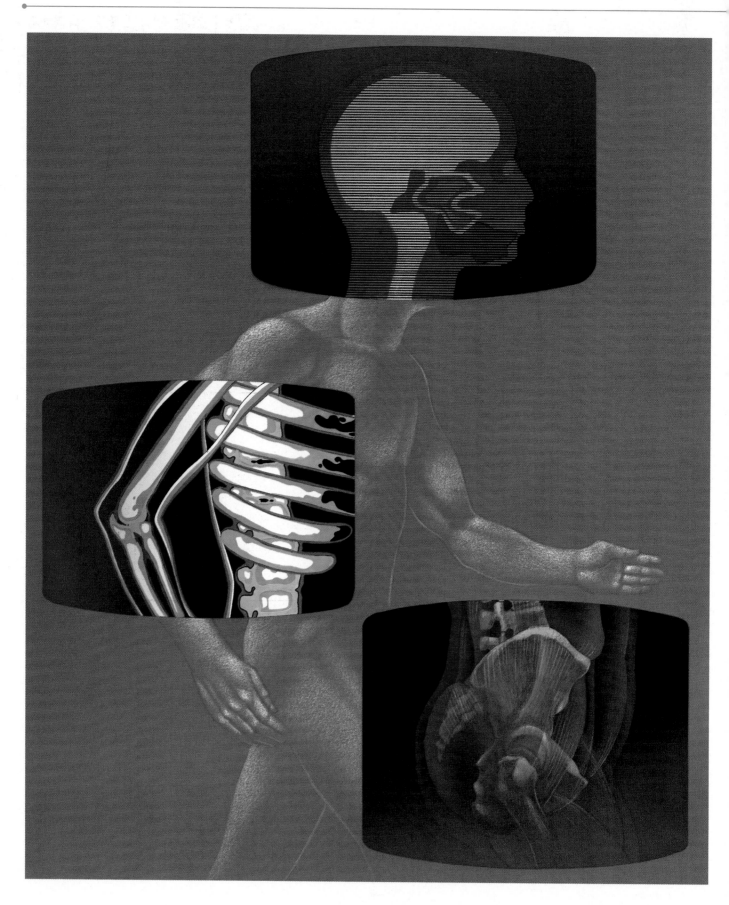

Plumbing the Body's Secrets

In 1967, a British electronics engineer with no training in biology or medicine had an inspiration that would profoundly change the study of the human organism. On a solitary weekend ramble through the English countryside, Godfrey Hounsfield hit upon the idea of hooking a computer to an x-ray machine. Hounsfield's mathematical investigations had led him to believe that the images produced by such a hybrid instrument would far surpass the standard, flat x-ray photographs in which organs, bones, and other tissues are represented by overlapping gray shadows.

Back in his lab at EMI, Ltd., an electronics and record-industry firm outside London, Hounsfield began feeding the output from a simple x-ray source into a bulky ICL1900 computer, a state-of-the-art machine that could store 200,000 words—impressive for the day. Having headed the team that in the late 1950s crafted Britain's first all-transistor computer, the EMIDEC 1100, Hounsfield was known as a superb engineer, even though he had never taken either master's or doctorate degrees. Given free rein by his employers and encouragement by the British Ministry of Health, he and his assistants put together a device that came to be known as the CT (for computerized tomography) scanner. The instrument would be heralded around the world as a boon to the understanding and exploration of the body.

THE UBIQUITOUS COMPUTER

Two decades after the lumbering prototype CT performed its first tests, computer technology has infused every aspect of medicine—from the chronicling of patient histories to the analysis of blood samples to the assessment of the relative severity of a patient's condition. In the emergency room, alongside the operating table, in the intensive-care unit, computers increase the speed and accuracy of treatment, take the guesswork out of surgery, and monitor vital signs with a vigilance that never flags. Their very ubiquity in the research laboratory would seem to make them unremarkable.

The rise of the microchip ranks as one of the most significant events in the history of medicine and biological research. As in the rest of science, computers represent not only another tool for learning but also a radical new approach to the pursuit of knowledge, one particularly suited to dealing with complex systems such as the human body.

Storing vast arrays of information far beyond the ability of the human brain to process, computers have spearheaded what the eminent physician and author Lewis Thomas has called "medicine's second revolution, which is transforming the profession from an art into a powerful and highly effective applied science."

At the most mundane level, microprocessors have simplified some of the day-to-day housekeeping chores of physicians—the recordkeeping, the management of information. But more important, microprocessors have extended the reach of the human intellect. Primed with appropriate programs, they discern underlying patterns that might not otherwise have been evident. Given, for instance, the complex electrical pulses generated by the heart and the brain, a computer can spot irregularities, signs of incipient disease that are too subtle to be seen merely in the wiggly output of the electrocardiogram or the electroencephalogram.

Computers have also greatly enhanced physicians' ability to diagnose patients rapidly and effectively. With a modem and a terminal, doctors can search databases such as MEDLINE for the latest published findings on a particular disease. Or drawing on software such as DXplain, PDQ, or ONCOCIN, they can review sets of symptoms and possible treatments, thus confirming or refining their own assessments. Someday, patients themselves might by similar means decide whether or not an ailment warrants a visit to a doctor.

ENABLING THE IMPAIRED

In the future, other interactive systems will ease the lives of the handicapped and impaired. Already, computer-designed prostheses far surpass those previously available. One prototype limb, an artificial arm and hand tied to nerves in the back, shoulder, and chest, and run by tiny motors, responds almost as if it were flesh and blood. A wearer has only to think about picking up an object for the bionic arm to swing into action.

Computer-linked voice synthesizers, wheelchairs, and other marvels of bioengineering have made it possible for people with birth defects, accidental injuries, or degenerative diseases to lead more productive lives. In the not-too-distant future, doctors may partly restore the vision of the blind and the hearing of the deaf by attaching miniaturized circuitry to their sensory nerves.

The most dazzling gains have come in imaging systems. By amplifying the powers of a range of existing instruments from microscopes to lasers, and by making feasible the invention of devices such as ultrasound and magnetic-resonance-imaging systems, computers have opened a new window on the body, offering researchers a fuller view of its workings—even the functioning of individual cells.

Yoked to sophisticated graphics software, supercomputers probe the architecture of vital molecules, including DNA, the convoluted stuff of heredity. As the intricate microscopic structures are laid bare, researchers gain a better understanding of how such molecules function and why they sometimes fail. On the larger scale, a host of computer-driven instruments now exist for translating signals from radioactive tracers, x-rays, radio waves, and even sound waves. Computers control the gathering of raw information, order the data according to mathematical instructions, and convert the results into graphic displays in two or three dimensions. Murky contours and shadowy recesses have given way to sharp, detailed images that can be brightened, enlarged, and otherwise enhanced with a keystroke. Without resorting to exploratory surgery or other invasive procedures, physicians can pinpoint tumors, track internal bleeding, or keep an eye on developing fetuses. Even the living brain, once the most inaccessible and unmapped region of the anatomy, springs into view on monitors, rendered in bright relief.

The latest-generation imaging systems outstrip their predecessors in speed and efficiency, in large measure because they have evolved with the computer. As computers have grown faster and more capacious, the resolution and versatility of imaging devices has increased. Whereas Godfrey Hounsfield's primitive CT machine took nine hours to do a scan and required an additional four days to analyze the data, a modern CT takes a couple of seconds to scan and gather up to two million separate pieces of data, which it assembles into an image less than a minute later.

Yet nearly every sophisticated imaging system in use today embodies techniques that Hounsfield applied in his first scanner. Although other scientists had sought to enhance x-ray images before, it was in Hounsfield's work that mathematical insight, engineering know-how, and inspiration came together in just the right combination.

Godfrey Hounsfield, whose shy, self-deprecating manner masks his scientific intensity, did not start out with the aim of revolutionizing medicine. In the early 1960s, after helping with the birth of the EMIDEC 1100, he instead focused on one of the thorniest problems faced by computer designers: giving computers the power of pattern recognition so that they could replace error-prone humans in such tedious jobs as inspecting industrial products. The challenge—not fully met even twenty years later—was to find a way to translate a picture of an object into the numerical language recognized and understood by a computer. The quest carried him into mathematical byways that led directly to the conception of the CT scanner.

The source of pictures for the computer's examination could be anything electronic—television, radar, or x-rays. Hounsfield's efforts ultimately converged on x-rays, widely used for quality-control inspection of precision parts —and, he quickly realized, for diagnosis of human injuries and ailments. But how could analog x-ray signals be transformed into digital copies of a three-dimensional object like the human body?

The solution lay in combining the insights of an obscure Austrian mathematician named Johann Radon with an x-ray technique developed by radiologists in the 1920s. Hounsfield speculated that by taking dozens of pictures of the body from different angles it would be possible, by carrying out an enormous number of repeated calculations, to reconstruct a cutaway view of the interior. Without a computer, the task verged on the impossible; even with one, it would be monumentally demanding. Hounsfield expected, though, that the images would far overmatch conventional ones.

A NEW USE FOR OLD MATH

The mathematical principles for reconstructing objects in this fashion had been discovered by Radon in 1917. Radon's transformation, as his proof is called, shows that from the infinite projections of an object—whether they are x-rays passing through it or light beams issuing from it—the object's features can be mathematically deduced. Uncirculated outside mathematical circles, the Austrian's work received little attention after its publication. However, several times during the following decades, radio astronomers and other scientists whose needs spurred them to study the reconstruction question independently replicated his results.

The x-ray technique developed in the 1920s was known as tomography, from the Greek for cutting or sectioning. Essentially it substituted physical motion for

Radon's mathematical analyses. By moving an x-ray beam in one direction, and an unexposed film in the opposite direction, radiologists obtained a picture, or projection, of a single slice of the body. By combining many pictures of the same slice, taken from different angles, radiologists could reconstruct a representation that was fuzzy but largely free of extraneous elements such as overlying bone, which cluttered normal x-ray photographs.

Hounsfield executed an elaborate variation on the tomographic theme and put the vast power of the computer to work on Radon's mathematics. Instead of photographic film, he used sensors that measured the strength of the x-ray beam after it penetrated the body; the signal strength, called a ray sum, provided a measurement of body density. When the beam passed through bone, which absorbs x-rays, the sensor measured a weak signal; when it passed through softer tissue, the signal was stronger.

Each exposure took hundreds of measurements of the patient's body density as it scanned horizontally across the edge of the selected slice. Then the ma-

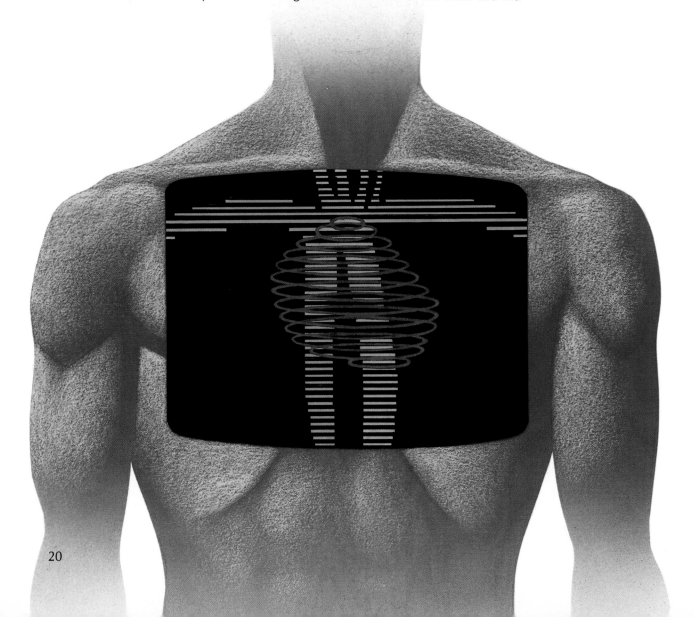

chine was rotated to take another series of measurements from a slightly different angle. The process was repeated scores of times until the patient had been completely encircled.

Drawn on paper, the beams' paths look like an extremely fine net; sets of parallel lines from each exposure intersect at slightly different angles. The lines' intersections are thousands of points; if the weight of each line corresponds to the strength of the signal it represents, some points become darker, and a picture emerges of that slice of the patient's body.

When this process takes place in a computer, the weight of each line becomes a numeric value in one of Radon's formulas. The weight of each point of intersection—now called a pixel, or picture element—is determined by hundreds of thousands of mathematical calculations, and the result, a remarkably detailed cross section of the patient's anatomy, is displayed on a video screen.

The computations, a process called algebraic reconstruction, required the computer to make a series of guesses for the actual density of each pixel, over and over again, each time making closer approximations based on the values of more recent guesses. Tying together all the pixels in the grid, the program gradually adjusted the values, as if it were solving a gigantic magic-square puzzle, until an equilibrium was reached, which signaled the completion of the reconstruction.

Technically, algebraic reconstruction requires an infinite number of ray sums to yield an image identical to the original. But by making certain mathematical compensations, Hounsfield was able to substantially reduce the number of readings needed. His prototype machine made do with 160 readings along each slice, and 180 around the body, forming a grid of 28,800 pixels.

Unbeknown to Hounsfield, another researcher working in the United States had already covered the same theoretical ground. In 1956, Allan Cormack, a South African nuclear physicist on sabbatical at the Cambridge Accelerator at Harvard University, concluded that reconstruction techniques could be used to considerably improve x-ray images. On his return to the University of Cape Town in 1957 he tested his notions, and after moving to the United States later that year, refined the mathematics and published his investigations in the *Journal of Applied Physics*. His work was not widely circulated, however, and it was left to Hounsfield to bring CT into being.

TINKERER'S TRIUMPH
Once he settled on the mathematics, Hounsfield constructed a machine that would provide him with the necessary data. Here, his talents as a tinkerer came in handy. Throughout his youth in England's Nottinghamshire farm country, he had fiddled with electronics, brewed up chemistry experiments, and engaged in primitive aeronautical design. (He made perilous flights on a homemade hang glider.) During and after the Second World War, Hounsfield had worked on radar systems, and after his graduation from Faraday House Electrical Engineering College in 1951, he carried on similar investigations for EMI's Central Research Laboratories.

Now, in 1971, he assembled a machine that allowed him to move an x-ray source along, as well as around, the body. On one arm of a U-shaped frame he mounted the source; on the other arm, directly opposite, a detector coupled to a device that boosted the final signal so it could be more easily deciphered by the ICL1900. Using a tiny aperture in a lead mask covering the x-ray source, he formed the x-rays into a pencil-thin beam, 1.5 millimeters wide. After each exposure, the beam was inched forward. The frame also rotated on a gantry allowing readings from 360 degrees. Because of mechanical constraints, the prototype was large enough only for studies of the head.

Moving quickly to tackle clinical problems, Hounsfield in 1972 scanned a woman patient thought to have a growth in her brain—a suspicion confirmed by the CT image, which revealed a cyst. Soon, the Atkinson-Morley Hospital in London was running a Hounsfield-designed CT and amassing a library of brain images. Word of the remarkable clarity of the views, which were up to 100 times better than ordinary x-ray film, spread rapidly through the medical research community, and late that year, the Mayo Clinic ordered a scanner from EMI, with special adaptations.

The machine arrived in March 1973, the first in the United States. Mayo radiologists immediately began using it to examine neurological patients, thus sparing them from undergoing pneumoencephalography, a painful procedure in which brain spaces were filled with air to increase the contrast between different types of tissue in an x-ray image.

After his remarkable success clarifying x-ray images, Hounsfield went on to investigate similar systems, exploring in particular nuclear magnetic resonance, later called magnetic resonance imaging. In 1979, at sixty, he shared the Nobel Prize in medicine with Cormack, whom he had never met or even heard of. In making the award, the Nobel committee cited the speed with which the CT scanner had "led to such remarkable advances in research and in a multitude of applications." By that time, CT had gained a prominent place on every major hospital's wish list. A decade later, the Mayo Clinic alone had fourteen CT scanners; its original machine was on display in the clinic's museum. More than 2,000 other scanners ran—sometimes ten to twelve hours a day, six days a week—in hospitals and research facilities nationwide, all bearing improvements in design and function.

A typical modern machine consists of a doughnut-shaped gantry holding a ring of 1,000 solid-state detectors. Patients slide through the hole in the doughnut on a motorized platform. The computer, tailor-made for the scanner and integrated

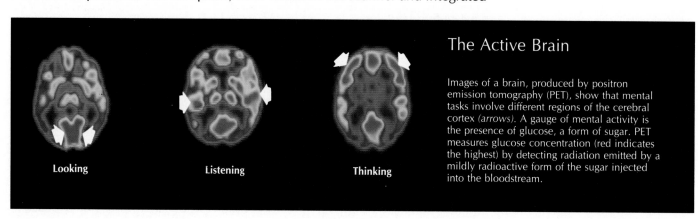

Looking

Listening

Thinking

The Active Brain

Images of a brain, produced by positron emission tomography (PET), show that mental tasks involve different regions of the cerebral cortex *(arrows)*. A gauge of mental activity is the presence of glucose, a form of sugar. PET measures glucose concentration (red indicates the highest) by detecting radiation emitted by a mildly radioactive form of the sugar injected into the bloodstream.

into its structure, choreographs a series of complicated maneuvers, rotating the gantry, regulating the voltage supply to the x-ray source, coordinating detectors, and storing 700,000 measurements per second.

NEW TECHNIQUES, NEW INSIGHTS

Still, CT scanners are not perfect. They expose patients to ionizing radiation—a potential hazard notwithstanding diminished exposure times. And although they reveal soft tissues, including tumors, with far more precision than conventional x-rays, it is still sometimes possible to miss tumors lying close to bone.

Magnetic resonance imaging solves both problems. MRI had been developed in 1948, but not until after Hounsfield's innovations was it practicable. In MRI, giant coils produce an intense magnetic field around a patient, aligning the body's hydrogen nuclei, which spin like tiny gyroscopes. A burst of radio waves sets the nuclei to wobbling at a predictable frequency, and when the nuclei settle back to their previous energy states, they give off radio waves, which sensors pick up and route to a computer, the indispensable element in the system. The waves pose no radiation hazards to patients or technicians. And they provide unmatched profiles of soft tissues. These tissues consist mostly of fluids, which, in turn, contain plenty of hydrogen atoms. By specifying different gradations from black to white, researchers can easily alter MRI images, bringing different tissue types to the fore and making bones vanish.

Another important system is ultrasound—a venerable idea but one that became practicable only with the rise of the computer. A kind of sonar for the body, ultrasound employs extremely high frequency sound waves—fifteen to fifty times beyond the highest frequency heard by humans. The waves penetrate the body, bouncing back when they hit boundaries—between tissues, for example, where fat meets muscle. A computer measures the echoes of the waves, then filters the signals and converts them into pictures.

Because the process takes place almost instantly—in so-called real time—it captures movement. This feature, and the fact that its sound waves are considered harmless to even the most delicate tissues, has made ultrasound a valuable way to monitor the development of fetuses. It also has been a boon in the study and treatment of heart disease and stroke. Whereas CT overlooks smaller blood vessels, ultrasound captures them in such detail that doctors can spot arteriosclerosis, or hardening of the arteries. Even the velocity of the blood in the neck is measurable, and for patients who have been stricken with brain aneurysms, such readings can forewarn of dangerous spasms—a common consequence of the illness, and one that can lead to death.

FROM DIAGNOSIS TO RESEARCH

In the mid-1970s, a third computer-driven imaging technique appeared poised to join the others as a key weapon in the diagnostic arsenal. Positron emission tomography, or PET, uses ionizing radiation to produce images of brain function. With PET, though, the radiation picked up by the sensors comes not from outside the body but from within. Natural substances, often glucose or glucoselike molecules, are tagged with radioactive markers and injected into the body. There they emit gamma radiation that can be detected, measured, and translated into an image by the computer.

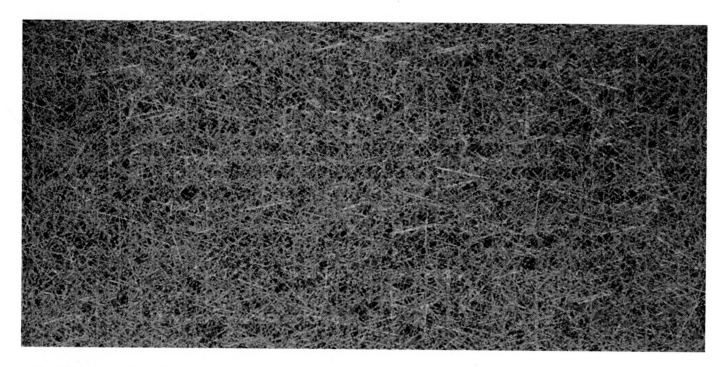

But PET proved less than ideal for the clinical setting. Its resolution is a poor match for CT or MRI, and the images were difficult to interpret. The equipment is also expensive and difficult to work with, owing to the nature of the radioactive markers used. These markers are deliberately made short-lived to reduce the possibility of injury to the patient. Their half-life is so brief—twenty minutes to two hours—that they must be custom-made each time the scanner is used. That means that each PET scanner has to have its own cyclotron, a smaller version of the particle accelerators used in atomic research. It soon became clear that other devices held more promise for diagnosis.

However, for researchers with the patience and wherewithal to deal with these difficulties, PET fulfilled a long-held dream of visualizing functioning cells. It was actually possible to watch on the monitor as the brain took up tagged molecules of energy-giving glucose. Biochemical maps of the shifting patterns of activity offered clues to the nature of the underlying tissues. Malignant tumors, for example, ravenously absorbed glucose. PET hinted at the underlying physical causes of schizophrenia and showed the damage wrought by Alzheimer's disease, or senile dementia, which previously was apparent only in autopsies or in experiments on animals with kindred pathologies.

THINKING MACHINES

Ever since the advent of the computer, philosophers and scientists have been intrigued by parallels between brains and the so-called thinking machines. The brain, it was said during the heady early days of artificial intelligence, was in fact a kind of computer. Neurophysiologists shied away from such simple comparisons. True, they said, both brains and computers process information, but in importantly dissimilar ways. Computers consist of orderly arrays of circuitry

Jumbles of lines represent links established between some 1,500 neurons in this two-part computer simulation of brain cells organizing to respond to a stimulus—an object sensed by nerves in the hand, for example. Colors represent connection strengths, yellow being the strongest, green average, and blue the weakest. Before stimulation *(left),* most cell connections are in the average range. After repeated stimulation *(right),* links between some cells have strengthened while others have weakened.

having only two states (on and off), and they carry out tasks in a serial fashion. The brain, on the other hand, is a tangle of 100 billion to a trillion neurons connected by more electrochemical pathways than can be counted. How these networks of nerves route and store information as well as trigger physical action and thought are among life's greatest mysteries.

By the mid-1980s, a more apt resemblance had been noted: The brain bears the same relationship to the mind (the thoughts, feelings, dreams) as a computer's hardware does to its software. "For the first time in history," said one cognitive scientist, "we have a relationship analogous to that between the brain and the mind. We can look to the computer and its software for help in explaining how minds, which are made of abstractions, can sit on top of brains, which are made of stuff."

The essential question of how the nonmaterial mind interacts with the material body has troubled Western philosophers from the time of the ancient Greeks. Plato put his stamp on the mind-brain problem, as it is now known, when he asserted that the mind and brain represent a duality, forever separate. In the seventeenth century, the French philosopher René Descartes elaborated this view, categorizing the mind as spiritual and the brain as physical.

Descartes and others formulated their notions with little reference to the actual "stuff" of the brain. Conversely, those who were studying the cells and structures of the brain hardly concerned themselves with speculative pursuits, concentrating instead on reconnoitering the territory. In 1718, the Dutch naturalist Anton van Leeuwenhoek slid thin pieces of the human brain under his microscope and was the first to see the brain's distinctive cell, the neuron, with its compact nucleus and long tail, or axon, ending in branching dendrites. Other researchers autopsied brains, mapping their complicated anatomy. By the late

Learning about Learning

The truth of the adage "practice makes perfect" is demonstrated every day: A toddler learns to tie a shoe; a grade-school student memorizes a multiplication table; an organist masters a Bach fugue. But how a human progresses from inept novice to nimble expert is—at the neurological level, anyway—a matter of considerable mystery.

Professor Gerald Edelman of the Neurosciences Institute at Rockefeller University in New York City theorizes that learning occurs because the neural connections involved in performing a task are strengthened by succeeding at it. The effect of such repetition is to establish the neural equivalent of an interstate highway for each learned activity.

Each human body is prewired with many billions of pathways having the potential to become interstates. The ones to undergo such improvement are chosen by a process that Edelman likens to the Darwinian concept of natural selection, at work in the evolution of species. That is, some pathways become better established than others, depending on how efficiently they perform a task.

To demonstrate his theory, Edelman and his colleagues at the Neurosciences Institute have programmed an IBM 3090 computer to acquire a simple discriminatory skill. The program is a simulation of a simple-minded creature that Edelman calls Darwin III. Its brain, consisting of 50,000 nerve cells connected by 620,000 synapses, is simpler than an insect's. Even so, within several hours of starting the program, the creature learns how to discriminate quickly and efficiently between objects in its presence. For this purpose, Edelman has given Darwin III a jointed arm ending in a "finger" that the creature can use to touch nearby objects, which it detects with a primitive "eye." Furthermore, Darwin III has innate abilities. Like any infant animal, it looks around its world, and it can move its arm.

Various kinds of objects may float into the creature's world. Some may be characterized by bumpy scallops around the edges, others by three black bar-shaped stripes in the center, and yet others by both features. Darwin III has a reflex response to expel from its presence any interloper having both bumps and stripes. Others it can ignore.

In early attempts to deal with an intruder, Darwin III's "eye roams like a newborn baby's in the dark," says Edelman. When an intruder enters the creature's peripheral vision, the computer program strengthens synapses between nerve cells that are active in the creature's simulated brain as the eye happens to move toward the interloper. This is accomplished by increasing the value of a number assigned to each synapse;

the number represents the strength of the connection. Synapses that are involved in moving the eye away from the intruder are reduced in strength. Similarly, the program reinforces arm movements and other exploratory behavior that lead to the identification and expulsion of noxious intruders. As subsequent interlopers appear, Darwin III seeks out the synapses with the highest values—that is, ones that have been used successfully in the past.

Darwin III's movements and brain activity are displayed on a computer monitor, as shown at right and on the following pages. After some 8,000 trials, the creature has become an expert. Darwin III's eye, instead of wandering aimlessly about the screen as it once did, turns quickly toward an intruder. The arm then reaches out to touch the object. Finding it to be striped and bumpy, the arm flicks the interloper away.

A new, inexperienced creature can be created simply by resetting the strengths of the nerve connections. But, says Edelman, "you can't predict how its brain will evolve, because it is not programmed." The particular nerve paths reinforced vary from one incarnation of Darwin III to the next, depending on the initial values assigned to the creature's synapses. Although it always learns to reject the bumpy, striped intruders, continues Edelman, it "develops its own individual way of ordering reality," just as the human brain does.

A simple electronic brain. Darwin III's world, appearing as a box in the upper left corner of the computer display at right, contains the creature's jointed arm, a red square outlining the field of view of its roving "eye," and an intruder (yellow shape). The rest of the display reports on activity inside Darwin III's brain, which consists of control centers for touch, eye movement, and arm movement. A fourth area, called the category-formation center, integrates visual and tactile information about an intruder to identify it. Numerous blue boxes within each center symbolize networks of nerve cells. Active cells appear as circles, some of which are visible in the eye-movement and arm-movement centers as Darwin III tracks and reaches out to touch an intruder. Large white circles signify the highest degree of activity; small blue circles are the least active cells. The four brightly colored squares dominating the eye-movement center represent nerve connections established as the creature learned how to turn its gaze toward an intruder.

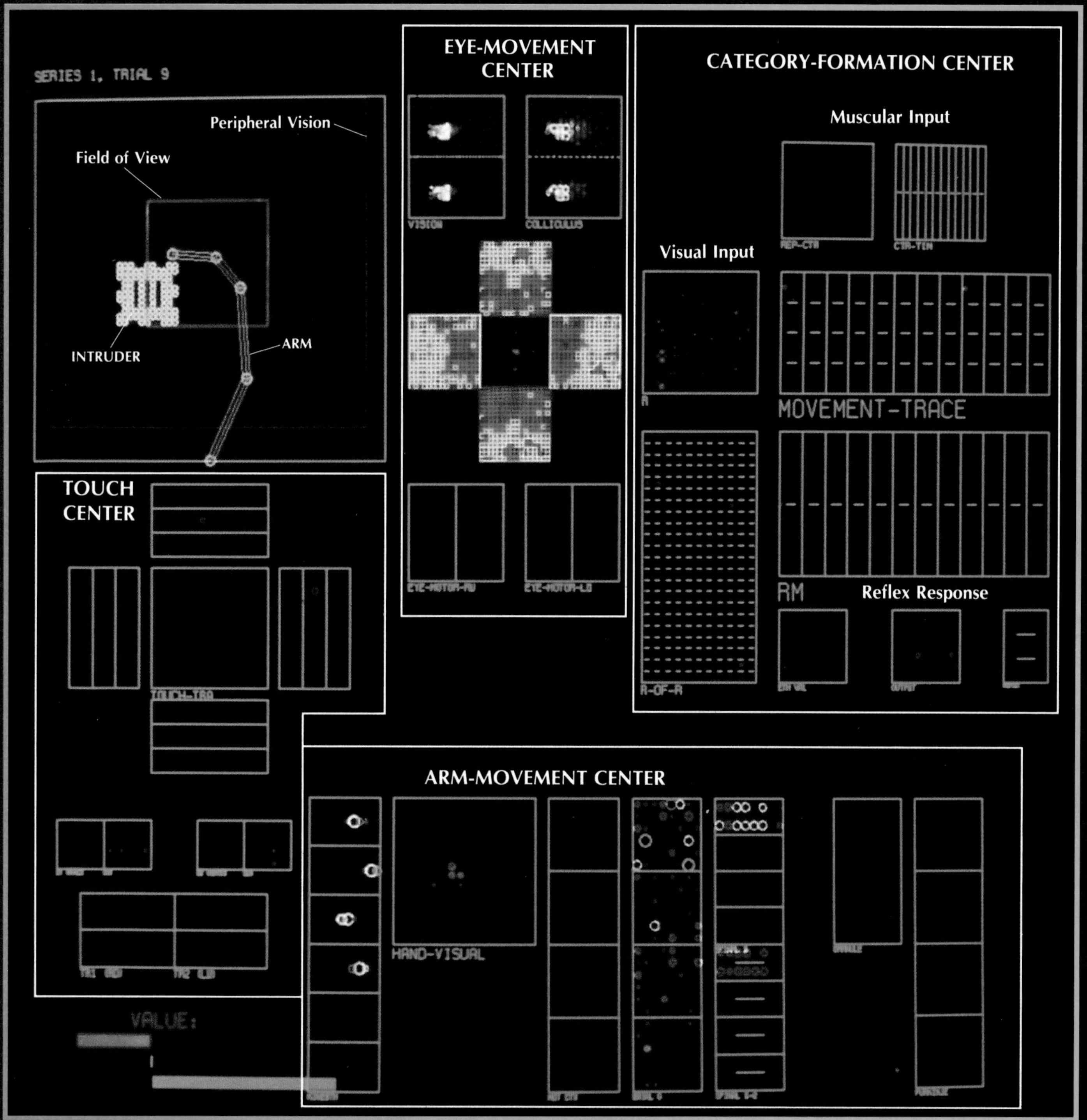

SERIES 1, TRIAL 9

Field of View

Peripheral Vision

INTRUDER

ARM

EYE-MOVEMENT CENTER

VISION

COLLICULUS

EYE-MOTOR-RU

EYE-MOTOR-LU

CATEGORY-FORMATION CENTER

Muscular Input

REP-CTR

CTR-TIN

Visual Input

R

MOVEMENT-TRACE

RM

Reflex Response

R-OF-R

OUT VAL

OUTPUT

REF

TOUCH CENTER

TOUCH-TRA

TR1 RU

TR2 LB

VALUE:

ARM-MOVEMENT CENTER

HAND-VISUAL

SPACE

SPACE 1-2

WHILE

VORTEX

1

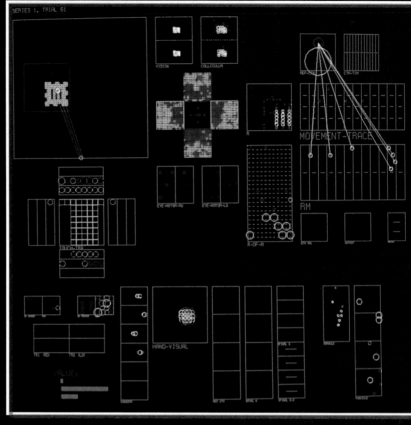

1

Probing an intruder. A white spot at the tip of Darwin III's arm, shortened to a single joint to save computing time, feels its way over the contours of an intruder. Here, nerve cells that sense muscular movements are actively stimulating *(white lines)* ones that sense the up-and-down motions of the arm, indicating the bumpy nature of the surface being traced. A yellow grid in the touch center represents the shape of the object as discovered by Darwin III. In the visual-input area, active nerve cells mimic the intruder's three dark stripes.

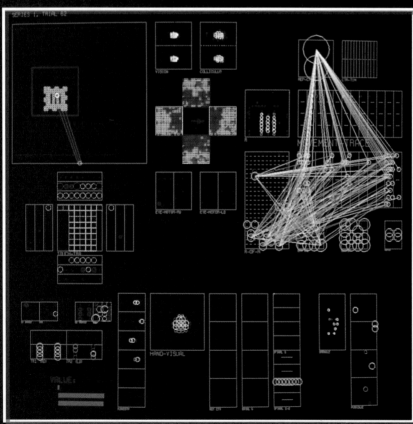

2

Comparing senses. The category-formation center explodes with activity as the creature correlates visual and tactile data about the intruder to confirm that it is both striped and bumpy. In the reflex-response region of Darwin III's brain, this description initiates the reaction appropriate for such an intruder—rejection.

3

Acting on reflex. Having appraised the intruder, Darwin III instantly recoils, causing nerve cells in the arm-movement center to light up. At the same time, nerve signals in the touch center cease, reflecting the arm's loss of contact with the intruder. Nerve cells in the visual-input area, however, continue to register the intruder's pattern of stripes.

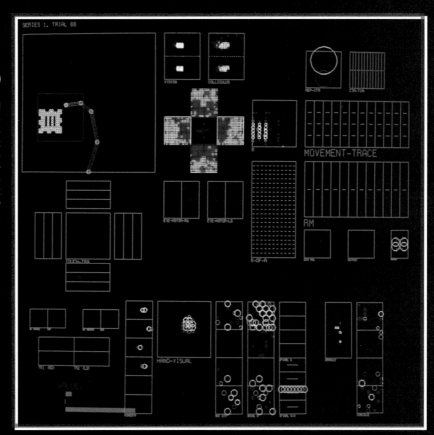

4

Rejecting the intruder. Darwin III pushes the intruder out of the blue box that defines the limits of the creature's world. The arm-movement center continues to show a high level of activity, but as the intruder is expelled, only one of its stripes remains in the visual-input area. After the intruder is gone, most nerve activity will cease—except in the eye-movement center, which directs Darwin III's eye in a systematic search for new intruders.

1800s, researchers had gained a greater understanding of the convoluted outer blanket of neurons called the cortex, and they knew that different portions of it were associated with phenomena such as speech and hearing.

From the nineteenth century onward, the dualistic stance steadily gave way to monism, the idea that all the activities recognized as "mind" arise from the continuous rush of electrical and chemical telegraphy in the brain. Most neuroscientists now embrace the monistic view and have begun to amass overwhelming evidence of its validity.

TOP-TO-BOTTOM KNOWLEDGE

Typically, brain researchers are cleft into two main groups, according to their starting point for study. Those who hold with the "bottom-up" approach attempt to stitch together a picture of the brain cell by cell. By microscopically examining stained or radioactively marked slivers of tissue, they have determined that the nerves in different parts of the brain release different chemicals to communicate with one another. To date, neuroscientists have identified several dozen such chemicals, called neurotransmitters. Practitioners of the bottom-up approach also measure electrical activity in individual nerve cells, threading thin wires called electrodes into them and recording their responses to external stimuli. Painstakingly, they assemble the whole from the parts. Those adopting the opposite, "top-down," approach opt for a broader attack. They record electrical activity across the whole brain as a person, say, performs simple tasks. Then they analyze the electroencephalograms mathematically, looking for overall patterns of activity.

Computer analysis of EEGs has already revealed that certain mental illnesses long regarded as purely psychological in origin in fact probably originate in physical anomalies. "Miswirings" in two specific regions of the cortex, for example, may account for the reading disorder dyslexia. Schizophrenia, too, may result from improperly formed nerve networks that impede the transmission of electrochemical signals. Further clues to mental illnesses come from computer-driven imaging systems, which pinpoint areas of the brain that exhibit high levels of cellular activity during various states such as sleeping, thinking, hallucinating, and dreaming. Homing in on specific sites where psychoactive drugs bind to nerves, researchers explore the links between brain chemistry and mental phenomena.

Arguably, the greatest contribution that computers have made to neuroscience has been to help draw a new portrait of the brain as a plastic, malleable organ that changes over time in response to its external environment. In the past, some scientists argued that the genes preprogram the growth of the nervous system, directing nerves to hook up in fixed patterns. In this view, nerve networks are hard-wired, like the central processing unit of a computer. But clearly the code contained in the DNA molecules inherited at birth does not absolutely specify the morphology, or shape, of an organism: Even identical twins do not look exactly alike.

In the late 1960s, Cyrus Levinthal, a biologist who started his career as a physicist, began pondering the role heredity plays in embryological development. To investigate the issues, Levinthal decided to chart the generation of nerves in lower-order species. The standard way of doing this was to remove the

Cyrus Levinthal of Columbia University is seen here with a computer reconstruction of a leech nerve cell created by his 3-D CARTOS imaging system. The neuron, outlined in purple, consists of a cell body and main branches (yellow), with smaller branches (blue) extending to sites where this cell connects to others (white). Detailed studies of simple nerve cells such as the leech's help scientists to develop models for the human nervous system.

brains of creatures such as the water flea or fruit fly at various stages of genesis, to encase the brains in paraffin or plastic, and to shave them into exceedingly thin slices that could be examined under the microscope. By comparing similar sections of a species' brain at different points in growth, researchers could chart when and how different nerves formed.

Envisioning the web of nerves from thin sections required a high degree of spatial imagination. Doing so was vital, though. "Whenever you're dealing with complicated three-dimensional structures," says Levinthal, "whether they are cells or groups of cells or nerve tracts running from one place to another, you have to be able to put that information into a three-dimensional framework in order to make it understandable."

Working at Columbia University in New York, Levinthal devised an imaging system that did just that. Boasting two display terminals, each equipped with a mouse, three microcomputers, and a variety of video equipment and other things, CARTOS—for computer-aided reconstruction by tracing of serial sections—allows researchers to produce moving pictures of cellular development as well as three-dimensional maps of bunches of nerves. "In simplest terms," says Levinthal, "CARTOS is a three-dimensional notebook." It records quantitative information about the size and shape of neurons, including the diameter of axons and angles of branching dendrites, and about the connections among groups of neurons.

To make a CARTOS model, researchers start with the basic thin slices used by earlier scientists, photographing them through light or electron microscopes. The resulting micrographs must then be aligned so that their true relationships are retained. This is done by eye, with the help of a computerized pattern-recognition system. Once they are aligned, the images are strung together on a device called an image combiner. The image combiner produces thirty-five-millimeter filmstrips that give viewers the illusion of tunneling through a mesh of interwoven nerves.

The next step takes hours of painstaking handwork, as researchers trace the outlines of pertinent details—whole nerves, points where nerves connect, or patterns of branching. Here, too, Levinthal and colleagues have simplified the task with a semiautomated tracer that aids in entering data into the computer. From this information—really a set of three-dimensional coordinates for every point on every feature that is of interest to the researcher—CARTOS mathematically reconstructs a picture that can be displayed on a television screen, magnified, disassembled, and otherwise manipulated.

Levinthal's CARTOS maps have revealed that, in general, a few simple rules govern the growth of nerves, and that the largest influence comes from surrounding tissues, whether other nerves or blood vessels. The final connections

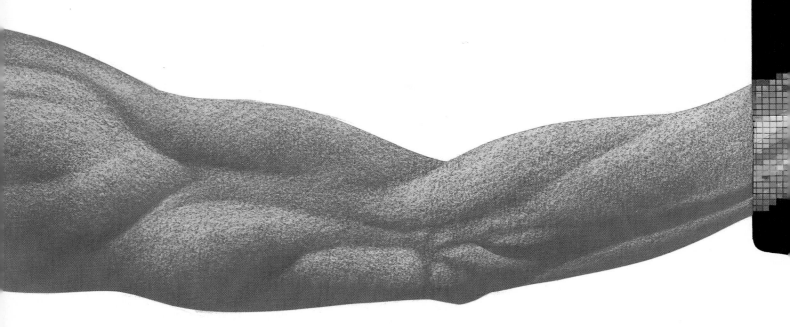

are not predetermined and always identical, but instead they vary to a lesser or greater degree among individuals in a species. Which genes, and how many, mastermind the growth of the nervous system is not yet clear.

ELECTRONIC NEURONS

Other researchers employing similar techniques have attempted to determine how the physical structures produce the distinctive patterns of electrical activity recorded on EEGs as well as trigger bodily movements. Using computers, researchers have learned to simulate networks of nerves. During the early days of computing, scientists aiming to expand the abilities of computers looked to brains for inspiration. One result was the Perceptron, a brainlike system designed to store information over grids, rather than at specific locations. But Perceptrons had major failings. The closer they came to resembling actual brains, the more sluggishly and dully they functioned. By the late 1960s, the notion of modeling computers after brains had fallen into disfavor.

In 1982, John Hopfield, a biophysicist with a joint appointment at the California Institute of Technology and Bell Laboratories, revived the idea, with a twist. Throwing in feedbacks, loops, and other mathematical arabesques, Hopfield created a system of equations that mimed the brain: It learned, it remembered, it forgot. It even occasionally overloaded and rid itself of unwanted memories.

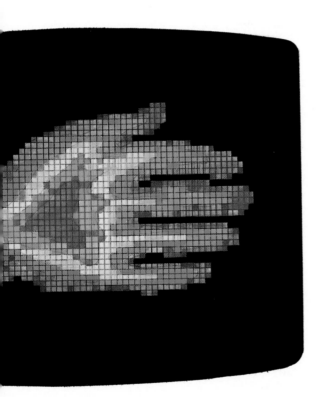

Capitalizing on Hopfield's discovery, other researchers moved from the crowded artificial-intelligence field to the study of neural networks. Fabricating a few hundred computer neurons, Terrence Sejnowski at Johns Hopkins and Charles Rosenberg at Princeton created a network that reads aloud. The computer recognizes letters and learns to identify corresponding sounds so that a voice synthesizer can speak them. At New York University, neuroscientist Rodolfo Llinas and his colleague Andras Pellionisz spent two years assembling two million artificial brain cells into a network that behaves like a cerebellum, the portion of the brain responsible for voluntary motion. The network, about the size of a frog's cerebellum, was randomly generated by the computer, which had memorized possible characteristics and configurations from several hundred real neurons. Stimulated by computer signals, the layered network produces electrical patterns matching those of a real brain. It also triggers motion in computer-drawn limbs.

In neural modeling, cross-pollination has been the norm. The new understanding of the brain feeds into computer design while the insights of twenty years of computing feed into neuroscience. Says one researcher, "The really hard problems are things the brain does well and a computer can't do at all. Vision, for example, and the understanding of speech. We are trying to build systems that do things like the brain does." The goal: computers that store memories over a cluster of chips, that never lose data catastrophically but only gradually, that modify old data as new data comes in.

Meanwhile, computer analyses emerging from the fledgling discipline known as chaos theory indicate that the brain, like the weather, operates on nonlinear principles. That is, each act strongly influences subsequent acts—but not in any predictable way. However, these chaotic acts are not random; they fall within the bounds of a general pattern of behavior. Explains Hopfield, "What you will be thinking a few minutes from now is extraordinarily sensitive to what went in a few minutes ago. And it's not possible to tell which of the relatively minor physical inputs may have a major impact on thought."

Such computer-gained knowledge is expected to provide new insights into the treatment of mental illness. Psychoactive drugs, such as thorazine for schizophrenia and others that counter depression, act on the brain in a direct but limited fashion, supplanting or suppressing single neurotransmitters or their chemical components. However, the organic bases of mental illness are thought to be far more complex—so complex as to almost defy comprehension.

If this is the case, the best hope for patients may be to determine the large-scale order hidden within seemingly random brain activity—a job for computers. Another potential solution is to ferret out the faulty genes that lead to mental and neurological illnesses. "Once identified as related to an illness," explains a National Institute of Mental Health assessment on neuroscience in the twenty-first century, "the gene can serve as a 'Rosetta stone' to decipher the molecular basis of that illness." In this latter endeavor, computers will prove indispensable.

DECODING DNA

Over the past three decades, a revolution has taken place in molecular biology, the field that scrutinizes proteins and DNA. Scientists have come to know more about the constitution and behavior of biological molecules than they have learned in all of history. For the most part, this knowledge has been gained only by a yeoman effort: endless hours of meticulous, repetitive experiment at the lab bench. Recently, though, the most wearying and rewarding of the molecular biologist's chores—unraveling the hereditary code carried in DNA—has been assumed by computers.

The earliest entry of computers into molecular biology came in the 1960s, when Cyrus Levinthal pioneered a technique known as molecular modeling (some five years before he devised CARTOS). At the time, Levinthal held an appointment at the Massachusetts Institute of Technology, where he was studying protein folding, the ways in which the long, twisted chains of amino acids that make up the protein molecules wrap around themselves to form the distinctive shapes that are critical to their function.

In those days, biologists trying to piece together a protein's unique structure relied in the main on x-ray crystallography, in which x-rays are passed through crystals of protein. The atoms in the protein bend the x-rays and appear as ghostly presences on an exposed film. From these films, researchers can roughly sketch out a molecule's form. Deciphering large protein molecules this way is extremely difficult, though, because they contain vast numbers of chemical bonds that fix the twisted amino acid chains in position.

A few days before Christmas 1964, Levinthal heard about a novel video imaging system that had been developed by M.I.T. colleagues; he became excited when he realized that, in theory, he could model proteins on it. Not more than a month later, he had learned enough of the programming language to run the system. Levinthal specified patterns of folding and bonding, based on his knowledge of the set angles and distances at which atoms of various sorts bind together. Then the computer assembled molecules in three dimensions and allowed them to be rotated and otherwise manipulated.

Using this system, Levinthal was able to probe the inextricable relationships between molecular shape and function. Neurotransmitters in the brain, for example, must dock at specific receptor sites on the nerve-cell membranes to do their work; only those molecules that have the right configuration fit the receptors. Similarly, antibodies, which thwart or kill invading bacteria or viruses, are shaped to latch onto the proteins that make up the outer coat of a germ. Shortly after he had mastered the computer at M.I.T., Levinthal was approached by pharmacologists who wanted to use the kind of interactive computer modeling he was developing to design more effective therapeutic drugs. When Levinthal moved to Columbia University, he wrote a computer graphics program that enabled him to move druglike molecules and proteins around on the same screen. If a sample drug molecule did not fit receptors on a protein, he could alter the drug molecule by selectively replacing amino acids, and the computer would automatically reconfigure it so a new test of fit with the target protein could be made. Today, it is common to subject new drugs to various tests on the screen before going into the lab to synthesize the real item and test its actual performance, an expensive and tedious process.

Around the time that Levinthal was toying with protein modeling, an explosion took place in an-

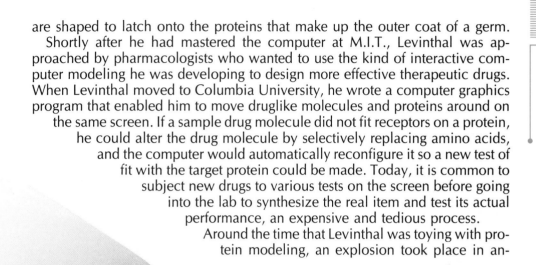

Cracking the Human Code

The most remarkable data-storage medium known to science is not a man-made creation but the natural substance that makes man: the double-spiral molecule known as DNA, for deoxyribonucleic acid. Within the nucleus of every human cell is the complete blueprint for an individual—approximately three billion units of information in forty-six chromosomes made out of DNA. This stupendous trove of genetic coding is known as the human genome. To decipher it, researchers are turning to the analytical and storage capabilities of another marvel of data handling—the computer.

A hierarchy of molecular relationships controls how cells

Inside a human cell. At the heart of every cell within the human body lies the nucleus, which contains forty-six chromosomes. No matter what the type of cell, these chromosomes hold all the genetic information necessary for the creation of an entire individual.

Into a chromosome. Each of the X-shaped chromosomes in a cell nucleus consists primarily of two long, intertwined strands of DNA, organized into informational units known as genes. Spread among all forty-six chromosomes are the 100,000 or so genes that code for the body's proteins and that are the main target of researchers' sequencing efforts.

function and thus how genetic traits are expressed. At the top of the list are proteins, which run virtually all the machinery of the human body and function according to shape. A protein's configuration is determined by the sequence of its building blocks, called amino acids. Each amino acid is itself the product of a sequence of chemical units known as bases, the fundamental constituents of DNA. Three successive bases constitute the code for one amino acid, and the full sequence of bases representing a protein constitutes a gene. Although DNA contains only four types of bases, the various triplet combinations of these bases direct production of twenty types of amino acids, which in turn create as many as 100,000 different proteins.

Deciphering the genome involves two tasks: determining the order of genes along the paired strands of DNA, and identifying each of the base pairs along these genes. The latter process, called sequencing, has until recently proved extremely tedious and expensive: A skilled lab technician, in effect working by hand, can sequence no more than 50,000 bases per year. But computer-assisted sequencing methods, such as the one explained on the following pages, can identify more than 15,000 bases in a single day.

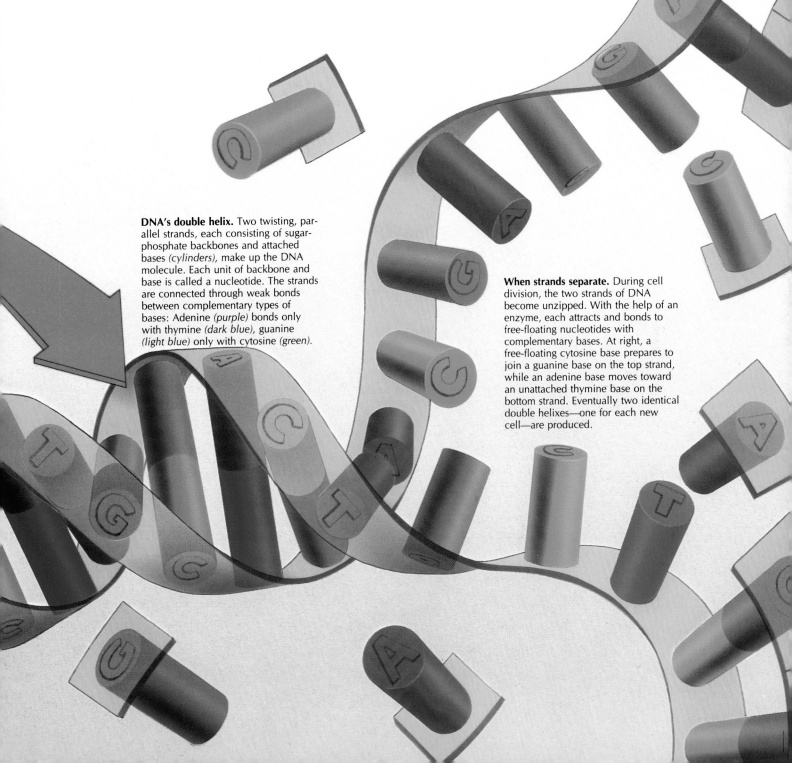

DNA's double helix. Two twisting, parallel strands, each consisting of sugar-phosphate backbones and attached bases *(cylinders)*, make up the DNA molecule. Each unit of backbone and base is called a nucleotide. The strands are connected through weak bonds between complementary types of bases: Adenine *(purple)* bonds only with thymine *(dark blue)*, guanine *(light blue)* only with cytosine *(green)*.

When strands separate. During cell division, the two strands of DNA become unzipped. With the help of an enzyme, each attracts and bonds to free-floating nucleotides with complementary bases. At right, a free-floating cytosine base prepares to join a guanine base on the top strand, while an adenine base moves toward an unattached thymine base on the bottom strand. Eventually two identical double helixes—one for each new cell—are produced.

A Recipe for Pinpointing Bases

Even in the simplified form shown here, automated gene sequencing involves a series of complex steps. To begin with, because a human gene can be several million bases long, it must first be chopped into manageable segments of a few hundred bases. Working with only one segment, researchers then create millions of identical copies and submit them to a process that results in further copies, ranging from one base long to the original segment's full length. Each of these pieces is tagged in such a way that a computer can identify its final base. In an ingenious last step *(pages 40-41)*, the pieces are

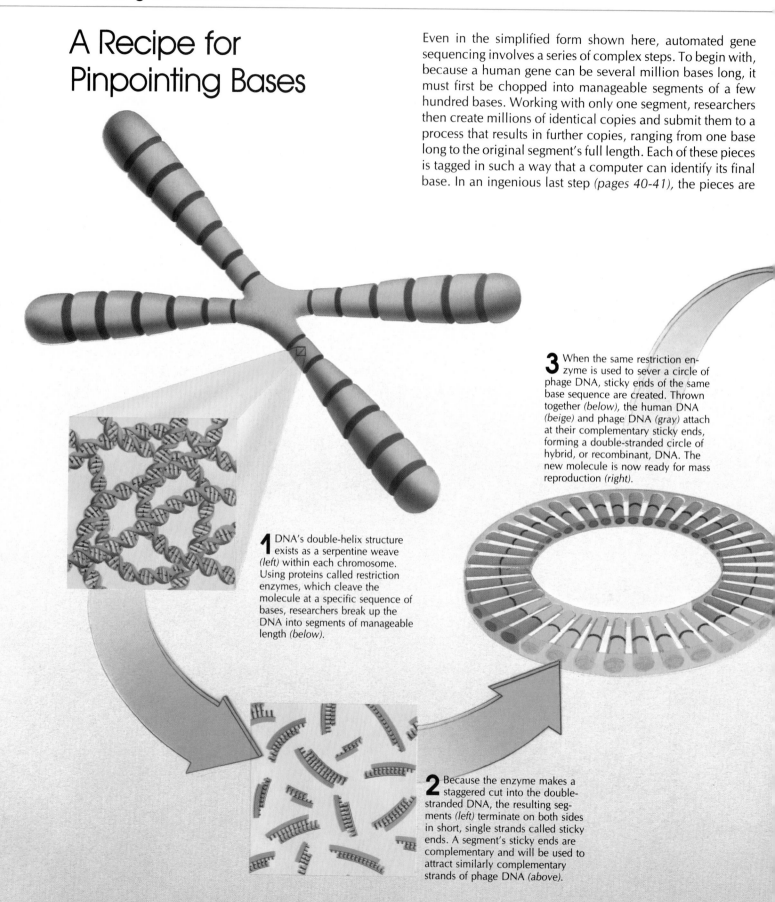

3 When the same restriction enzyme is used to sever a circle of phage DNA, sticky ends of the same base sequence are created. Thrown together *(below)*, the human DNA *(beige)* and phage DNA *(gray)* attach at their complementary sticky ends, forming a double-stranded circle of hybrid, or recombinant, DNA. The new molecule is now ready for mass reproduction *(right)*.

1 DNA's double-helix structure exists as a serpentine weave *(left)* within each chromosome. Using proteins called restriction enzymes, which cleave the molecule at a specific sequence of bases, researchers break up the DNA into segments of manageable length *(below)*.

2 Because the enzyme makes a staggered cut into the double-stranded DNA, the resulting segments *(left)* terminate on both sides in short, single strands called sticky ends. A segment's sticky ends are complementary and will be used to attract similarly complementary strands of phage DNA *(above)*.

organized from shortest to longest, and the computer examines each one in turn, noting the final base and thereby determining the complete sequence.

Creating copies, or cloning a segment, requires the services of a type of virus called a phage. Like all viruses, a phage is little more than a circle of DNA that reproduces rapidly after injecting itself into a host cell, typically a bacterium. Inserting a piece of human DNA into a phage thus automatically generates the millions of copies necessary for sequencing.

Split into single strands, these copies are divided among four chemical soups, each containing chemical agents known as primers, which are marked with fluorescent dye that corresponds to one of the four types of bases. The primers are specially designed to latch on at the junction of the human DNA and initiate the attachment of free-floating nucleotides that will create a new strand. Each soup also contains one type of "false" nucleotide that will prevent further attaching, so that all new strands will end with the same base. Because the false bases attach randomly at different positions (below), the new strands vary in length, setting the stage for the final step.

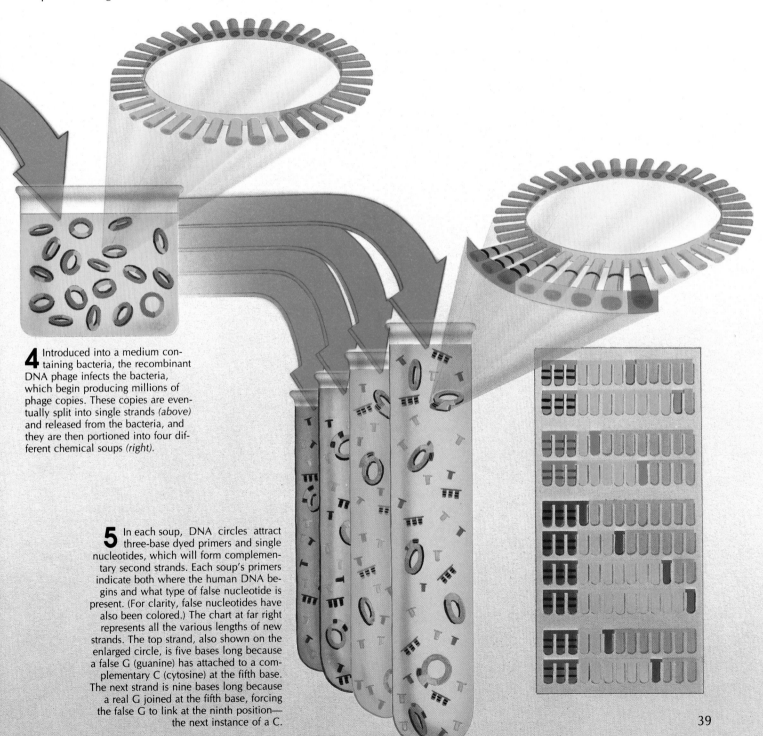

4 Introduced into a medium containing bacteria, the recombinant DNA phage infects the bacteria, which begin producing millions of phage copies. These copies are eventually split into single strands (above) and released from the bacteria, and they are then portioned into four different chemical soups (right).

5 In each soup, DNA circles attract three-base dyed primers and single nucleotides, which will form complementary second strands. Each soup's primers indicate both where the human DNA begins and what type of false nucleotide is present. (For clarity, false nucleotides have also been colored.) The chart at far right represents all the various lengths of new strands. The top strand, also shown on the enlarged circle, is five bases long because a false G (guanine) has attached to a complementary C (cytosine) at the fifth base. The next strand is nine bases long because a real G joined at the fifth base, forcing the false G to link at the ninth position—the next instance of a C.

Shedding Light on Base Order

1 In this simplified example of an automatic sequencer, the contents of all four soups have been combined and poured onto a single lane of gel. Because the top of the gel is negatively charged and the bottom positively charged, the DNA fragments, which carry a negative charge, migrate through the gel toward the bottom. Since the smaller fragments travel faster, the field naturally separates into bands, each containing fragments of the same length, which end with the same type of final base.

2 As each band migrates toward the bottom of the gel, it passes through a laser beam that excites the fluorescent dye that marks that band's fragments. Here, the beam strikes the fourth band, causing it to radiate light at a frequency in the purple color range.

Although far too small and numerous to be easily identified and organized by even the most skilled laboratory worker, the millions of DNA pieces floating in the four chemical soups quickly reveal their secrets to the computerized genome-sequencing system. The sequencing process described here is run by a single microprocessor and employs nothing more powerful than a personal computer to translate and store the fragments' data.

The first sequencing step, to arrange the pieces in order of length, relies on a device basically consisting of a slab of gel sandwiched between two glass plates (left). Through positive and negative charging of the gel, which influences the movement of the negatively charged fragments, all the DNA strands are separated into bands of different lengths, arranged from shortest to longest and color-coded according to their terminating base. (The sequencer here has been simplified for clarity; an actual sequencer would consist of sixteen sequencing lanes, rather than just one, and would handle roughly ten million, rather than ten, individual pieces of DNA.)

A series of other devices, including a laser beam, a color wheel, and a photomultiplier, enables the computer to identify the terminating base of every band, each of which corresponds to a single base on the original gene segment. This information is stored in digital form on a hard disk. The process repeats for each of the thousands of original segments until the base sequence for an entire gene has been described.

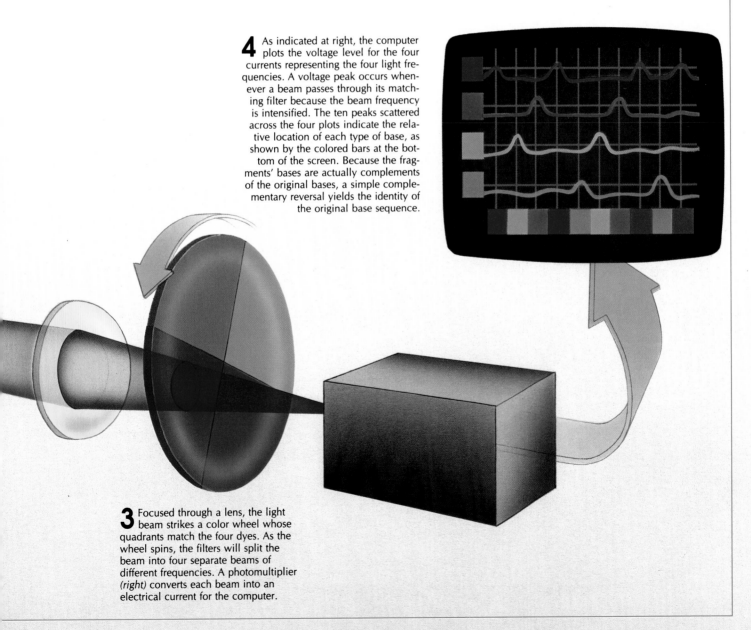

4 As indicated at right, the computer plots the voltage level for the four currents representing the four light frequencies. A voltage peak occurs whenever a beam passes through its matching filter because the beam frequency is intensified. The ten peaks scattered across the four plots indicate the relative location of each type of base, as shown by the colored bars at the bottom of the screen. Because the fragments' bases are actually complements of the original bases, a simple complementary reversal yields the identity of the original base sequence.

3 Focused through a lens, the light beam strikes a color wheel whose quadrants match the four dyes. As the wheel spins, the filters will split the beam into four separate beams of different frequencies. A photomultiplier (right) converts each beam into an electrical current for the computer.

other area of molecular biology, the study of DNA. Francis Crick, James Watson, and Maurice Wilkins had shared a 1962 Nobel Prize for discovering the structure of DNA. By the mid-1970s, scientists had a clear picture of how these long, spiraling ladders of phosphates, sugars, and elemental matter directed the manufacture of vital proteins. There began a rush to decode DNA from humans and other creatures, primarily to gain a greater fundamental understanding of the molecular basis of life. Only in the mid-1980s, though, could scientists dream of deciphering the entire human genome, the 100,000 to 300,000 genes contained in the forty-six chromosomes inherited at birth—all because of the computer. Without the computer, the job, which has been dubbed the holy grail of human genetics, might take a century or longer; with it, perhaps thirty years.

The smallest human chromosome contains about 5,000 genes, which are simply segments of DNA. They carry the instructions that enable the cellular machinery to produce a specific protein. Genes, in turn, contain sequences of four compounds, the bases adenine (A), thymine (T), guanine (G), and cytosine (C). These four bases, pairs of which make up the rungs of the spiraling DNA ladder—the double helix described by Crick, Watson, and Wilkins—are the letters in the DNA code.

The sequence of these base pairs dictates precisely how protein chains will be assembled. The sequence GTG, for example, tells the cell to add the amino acid valine onto a growing protein chain; TTG, to add leucine. Each of the twenty amino acids is represented by one or more three-letter combinations—called codons—that signal its addition to the chain.

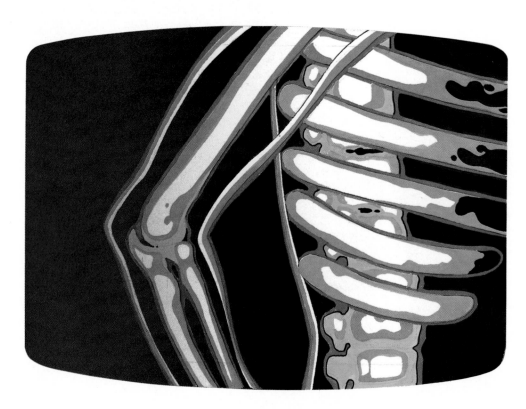

For most of the last fifteen years, breaking the genetic code has been costly, labor-intensive, and achingly slow. Radioactively labeled DNA had to be chemically chopped up and the fragments passed through a slab of gel polarized by an electric current. After several other steps, the sequence of a short section of the DNA could be puzzled out. To obtain the code for even a small gene might take three or four months. A good technician could sequence a maximum of 50,000 base pairs a year.

SORTING THE SEQUENCES

In 1986, Leroy Hood, a biologist at the California Institute of Technology, changed all that. No tyro at instrument design, Hood had in 1975 devised a machine for determining the sequence of amino acids in proteins. Soon afterward, he built another, for putting together short pieces of DNA, and yet another for assembling proteins outside of cells. Now, he turned the computer loose on DNA sequencing.

Working with several other researchers, Hood invented a computer-driven instrument that can sequence more than 15,000 base pairs per day. The automated sequencing machine, called the DNA Sequenator, attaches fluorescent dyes to DNA fragments, one color for each of the four bases. As the fragments pass through an electrically polarized gel, a laser excites the dyes, and a sensor reads the various colors, marking their passage and enabling the computer to identify and chart the fragments. The signals are stored on a twenty-megabyte hard disk. Sorting this data, the computer determines, with 98 to 99 percent accuracy, the order of the base pairs along the original strand (pages 36-41).

Much of any string of DNA consists of "junk" sequences or, more accurately, those with no currently discernible function. Thus, the most important aspect of sequencing is finding those stretches of code that are known to be important, and setting aside the rest for later study. Computers, with their ability to scan long strings of base pairs seeking patterns and comparing different groups, now help winnow out those that are meaningful. Programs that run on personal computers hunt for series of bases that have in the past been associated with genes, sparing researchers tedious manual searches.

Simpler programs manage the enormous library of known sequences, now extending to 10 million base pairs or more. Two databases set up in 1982, one in Heidelberg, Germany, at the European Molecular Biology Laboratory, and one in Los Alamos, New Mexico, at the U.S. National Laboratories, can be accessed by commercially available software. An electronic clearinghouse, BIONET, affords molecular biologists a forum for the speedy exchange of information.

Even so, the masses of data generated by molecular biologists each year overwhelm current arrangements. At both Heidelberg and Los Alamos, there are typically backlogs of sequences waiting to be entered into the system by hand. Manually typing page after page of code is mind-numbingly slow, and the likelihood of typographical errors is high. Automated sequencing equipment, however, creates computer-readable records that can be sent to the data banks on magnetic tapes. Hood and others predict that advanced technology will make other aspects of managing DNA data simpler: Parallel processors and supercomputers will speed analysis, and advanced software will help recognize genes more surely.

Many biologists are pushing for a more ambitious data-collection effort: They want to sequence the entire human genome, a goal that has sparked controversy within the community since it was first discussed publicly in 1985. The sticking point is the enormous scale of the project.

Costs could run to $200 million each year, with the final bill totaling $500 million to $3 billion. Opponents question whether so much money and effort should be diverted from other areas of biological research for a project of questionable final worth. Proponents such as Hood admit, "A full-scale sequencing effort launched now, with existing technologies, would indeed be expensive and time-consuming. But the costs can be reduced if we first develop and optimize the appropriate automated technologies." Many scientists believe the benefits justify the cost. Already, computer-assisted searches have yielded the genes that cause three wasting ailments—Huntington's disease, cystic fibrosis, and muscular dystrophy; and researchers are hot on the trail of defective genes responsible for other inherited diseases. Although the identification of these genes does not guarantee a cure for the diseases, it does permit early and rapid diagnosis—and it provides the basic information needed to search for a way to prevent them.

Once the entire genome is mapped, computers could be used for a variety of purposes. By comparing human DNA sequences to those of other animals, computers could reveal genes that have remained virtually unchanged over millenniums, thus elucidating the microbiological underpinnings of evolution. Or computer scrutiny could disclose sequences similar to those displayed by cancerous cells, giving further clues about how certain proteins prod healthy cells to run amok. Already, similar searches have led investigators to greater understanding of the AIDS virus. Various computer-linked equipment has helped zero in on the docking site where the virus attacks the immune system's T-4 cells, thus opening the way for the development of vaccines and drugs to thwart and treat the disease.

Sequencing the human genome, like mapping the brain and the body, promises to carry biologists across unscouted frontiers and to yield insights that may one day help eliminate ancient scourges—cancer, mental illnesses, inherited diseases. Computers will help decipher these mysteries, as they have for the past thirty years. If the human organism—its feedbacks, interrelationships, and governance—is as complicated as the first generation of advanced instruments have hinted, then the continually evolving computer stands as the only bridge to the realms currently beyond the reach of the unaided intellect.

Clear Views
of the Interior

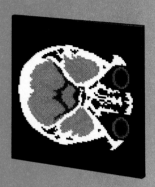

Before computers, all medical techniques used for looking inside the body had a serious shortcoming. Whether the medium was x-rays, high-frequency sound, or the faint emission of gamma rays from a mildly radioactive chemical injected into the body, the photographic images produced were devoid of depth. They showed not one organ behind another, but all of them merged together, front to back, into a single plane of shadowy forms and indistinct shapes.

For decades, scientists have understood the principles that would permit construction of medical-imaging equipment that could overcome this obstacle—in theory. As a practical matter, however, their ideas required mathematical calculation on a scale that only a computer could manage.

In general, the computer makes two things possible. First, it permits a doctor to view a patient as if drawn in cross section. The tissue lying in front of the plane of the cross section is excluded, as is the tissue behind it. The result is an unambiguous image that even a layman can appreciate; moreover, the computer can create a cross-sectional image through any point on the body and at any angle. Second, the computer gives a doctor the choice of emphasizing some tissues in an image at the expense of others simply by turning a few knobs on a computer console. A physician attempting to get a clear view of a suspicious growth, for example, can tell the computer to remove other tissue from the image.

Since the 1970s, computers have been linked with x-rays in a technique called computed tomography (CT), with high-frequency sound to produce ultrasonic images of remarkable clarity, and with radiation from the disintegration of atomic nuclei. In addition, computers have made possible a new technique called magnetic resonance imaging, which produces something never before possible: clear, detailed images of the body's soft tissues.

Digitized Layers of Anatomy

Computerized medical-imaging equipment presents views of the body as if it were made of thin layers or slices. A physician can choose to study any layer in isolation from all the others, whereas noncomputerized approaches, in effect, treat the entire thickness of the body as a single slice. Such inclusiveness exacts a high informational price. Internal organs and structures are mere shadows of the real thing. Soft tissue, often obscured by bone, can be especially difficult to see.

Points of view. Planes passing through a model of a human head *(below)* illustrate the variety of cross-sectional slices that computerized imaging techniques can produce. Each plane can be shifted to positions alongside the ones shown here or, as in the case of the inclined plane, rotated to produce an angled view.

A frontal slice. This cross section of the head taken vertically, just in front of the ears, shows the brain enclosed by a dark layer that represents the skull. The white layer outside the skull is skin and fat.

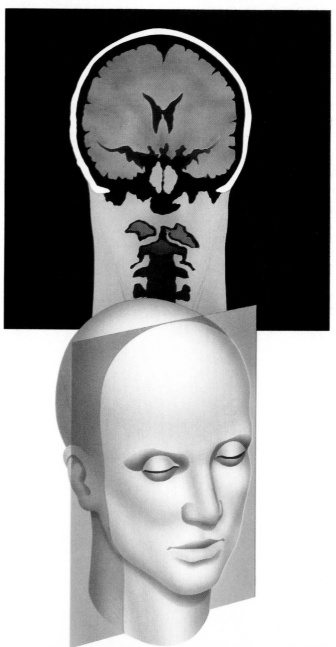

To expose the interior of the body for the purpose of diagnosis, computerized imaging gear can slice the human body in virtually any direction, though not always with equal facility. For example, magnetic-resonance-imaging equipment *(pages 56-57)* can be adjusted to produce all three of the primary types of slices shown below.

By contrast, a computed-tomography installation, as explained on pages 50-51, generally produces only transverse slices. Other kinds of CT slices are possible, but demanding in scanner and computer time.

For a skilled diagnostician, the opportunity to display parts of the body from exactly the right angle can mean the difference between estimating and actually seeing the nature and extent of many ailments, from the precise location and size of a tumor to the extent of a hemorrhage or the gravity of a muscle tear.

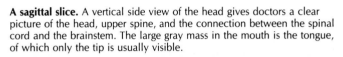

A transverse slice. Passing a plane horizontally through the head at eye level reveals the orbs of the eyes, which appear to be held alongside the nasal passages in the pincerlike grip of the heavy bone that surrounds and protects the eyes.

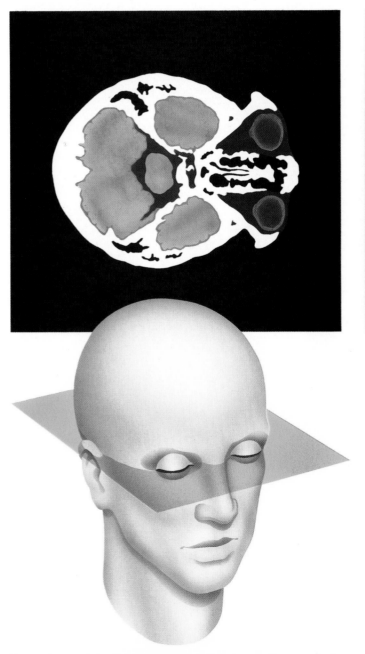

A sagittal slice. A vertical side view of the head gives doctors a clear picture of the head, upper spine, and the connection between the spinal cord and the brainstem. The large gray mass in the mouth is the tongue, of which only the tip is usually visible.

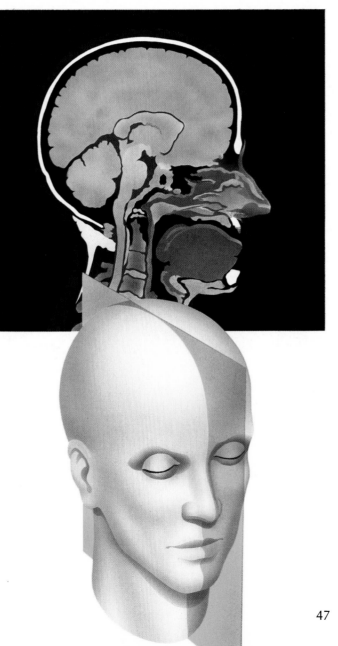

Images from Tiny Bricks of Data

Any computer-generated image of the body is a pattern of data fragments called volume elements, or voxels. As shown below, a voxel has a square end, each side typically measuring one millimeter. Its length—the thickness of the slice—commonly lies between two millimeters and ten millimeters. Each voxel represents a three-dimensional section of tissue at a specific point in the body.

During imaging, a voxel takes on a numerical value denoting both its location and the effects of the tissue there—the

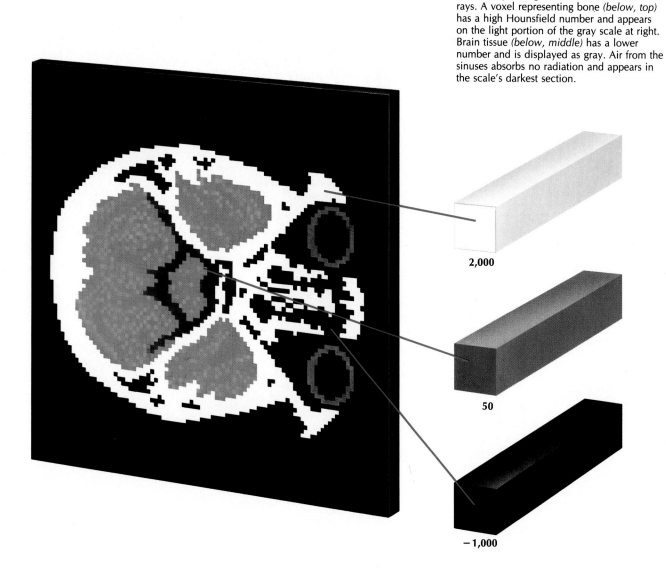

This transverse CT image of a human head is a mosaic of black, white, and gray voxels shaded depending on their resistance to x-rays. A voxel representing bone (below, top) has a high Hounsfield number and appears on the light portion of the gray scale at right. Brain tissue (below, middle) has a lower number and is displayed as gray. Air from the sinuses absorbs no radiation and appears in the scale's darkest section.

2,000

50

−1,000

amount of radiation absorbed or emitted, the size of an ultrasonic reflection, or the frequency of an emitted radio signal. To display an image, the computer selects voxels for assembly into a mosaic of the slice through the body that a doctor wishes to examine.

Much of computer imaging's versatility resides in a provision for temporarily changing the color or gray tone assigned to voxels in the mosaic. Called windowing, this feature permits a doctor to clarify the view of some types of tissue at the expense of detail in others. The principle is explained here by means of the Hounsfield scale (below, left), a display methodology used in computed-tomography scanning and named for the technique's inventor. Hounsfield numbers, ranging from −1,000 for tissues most easily penetrated by x-rays to +3,000 for the most opaque types of bone, can be assigned to one of 256 shades of gray to create an image. Through windowing, a physician can assign all 256 tones to a portion of the scale to emphasize tissues of particular interest.

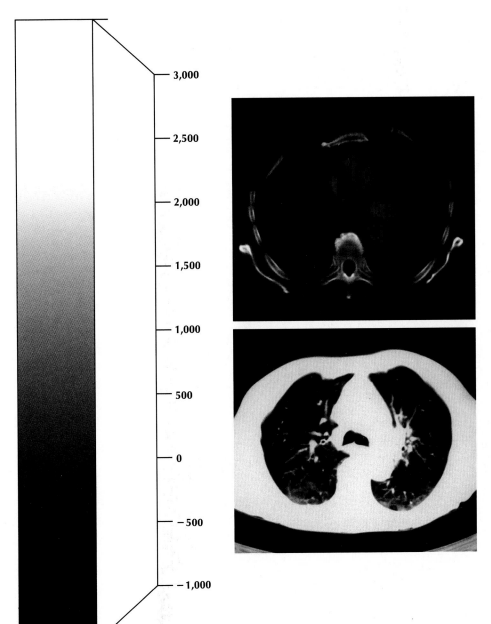

3,000

2,500

2,000

1,500

1,000

500

0

−500

−1,000

Emphasizing soft tissues. For this transverse slice of a chest taken just above the heart, the bottom of the window was set at 115 and upper limit at 155. In the center of the image, flanked by the black voids of the lungs, are the heart's major blood vessels. The smaller black shape is the trachea. Because of the setting, the calcified outer layers of bones— breastbone, ribs, shoulder blades, and a vertebra—appear white. Layers of muscle and fat are visible around the periphery of the body.

Details of the lungs. The soft tissues in the image above are turned white by setting the bottom of the window at −1,000 and the top at −325. Although the trachea, containing only air, remains black, lung tissue now appears as a dark gray tone with a white network of blood vessels.

49

Dispelling the Murk from X-Ray Images

Shadows cast by sunshine reveal no more about the shapes and arrangement of chairs on a lawn than a single x-ray image reveals about the shapes and arrangement of organs in the body. Physicians deal with the situation by positioning a patient in front of a conventional x-ray machine in a way that will produce the clearest image of the organs and structures under scrutiny.

If the body—or the lawn chairs—were illuminated from many directions, one at a time, each of the resulting shadows

Preparing a slice. A single rotation of a CT scanner's x-ray tube and detectors supplies all the data needed for a computer to display a transverse slice of internal organs and structures. Between scans, a motorized pallet advances the patient a short distance in preparation for the next slice.

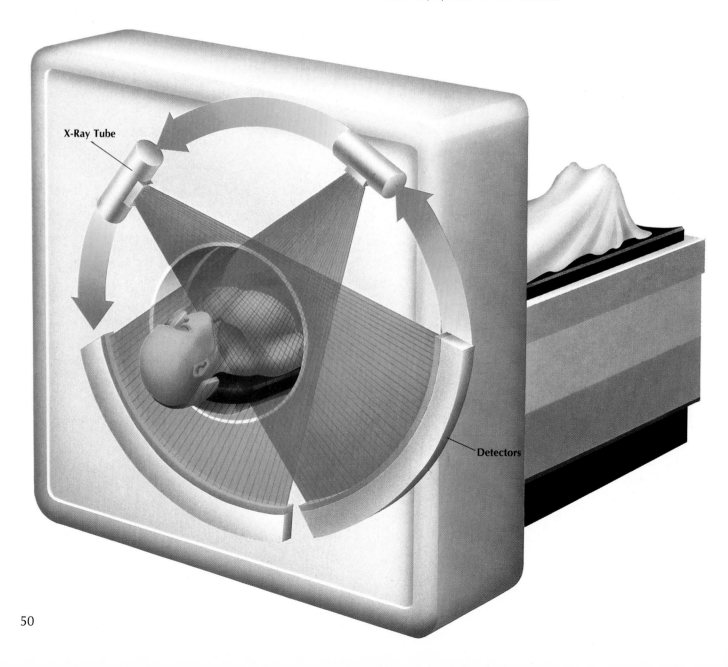

X-Ray Tube

Detectors

would contain an additional measure of information about the true shape of the object being investigated. But dividing the whole from the parts is simply beyond the capabilities of the human brain.

Computed tomography uses a computer to assemble the pieces. As shown on the preceding page, CT scanning equipment projects a beam from a rotating x-ray tube. Each ray of the beam, passing through the patient, is partially absorbed by the tissues in its path. The intensity of the emerging ray is measured by a narrow detector, opposite the tube, that converts the radiation into a digital electrical signal and sends it to a computer for storage.

The equipment makes x-ray exposures of thin slices of the body from hundreds of different angles. Each slice requires up to ten seconds to scan; a full CT scan of the abdomen requires about fifteen slices and takes several minutes. Once the data is collected, the computer can display any transverse slice in a matter of seconds.

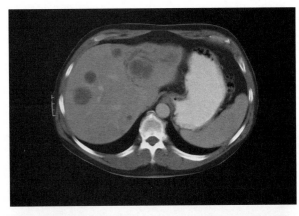

A view of the abdomen. The large gray mass in this CT image is the liver; dark spots indicate less-dense tissue, possibly tumors. To the right of the liver is the stomach. Denser than the liver, it is relatively opaque to x-rays, giving it a tone nearly as light as that of the spinal column at the bottom of the image and the ribs at the perimeter. The long gray shape next to the stomach is the spleen.

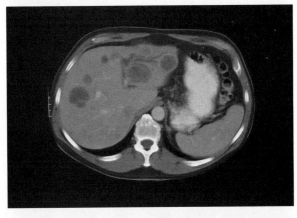

A few slices lower. Another view taken below the first shows the same major features but also reveals part of the colon, visible between the spleen and stomach as black circular shapes outlined in gray. The interior of the colon is black in the image because it is filled with gas, which is completely transparent to x-rays.

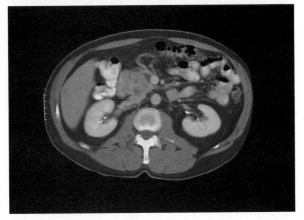

At the midpoint. In this image, taken roughly at the middle of the abdomen, the kidneys become visible and the intestines even more prominent. The gray area surrounding the spine indicates the supportive, protective muscles of the lower back.

By the Light of Gamma Rays

The flow of blood or the concentration of chemicals in an organ or tissue can be a clue to its health. Mild radioactivity can make such indicators visible. For example, potassium collects in the heart, where it helps assure a steady heartbeat. Radioactive thallium, a close chemical relative of potassium, will also accumulate there, and indirectly, it can reveal if the heart is receiving an adequate supply of oxygen-rich blood.

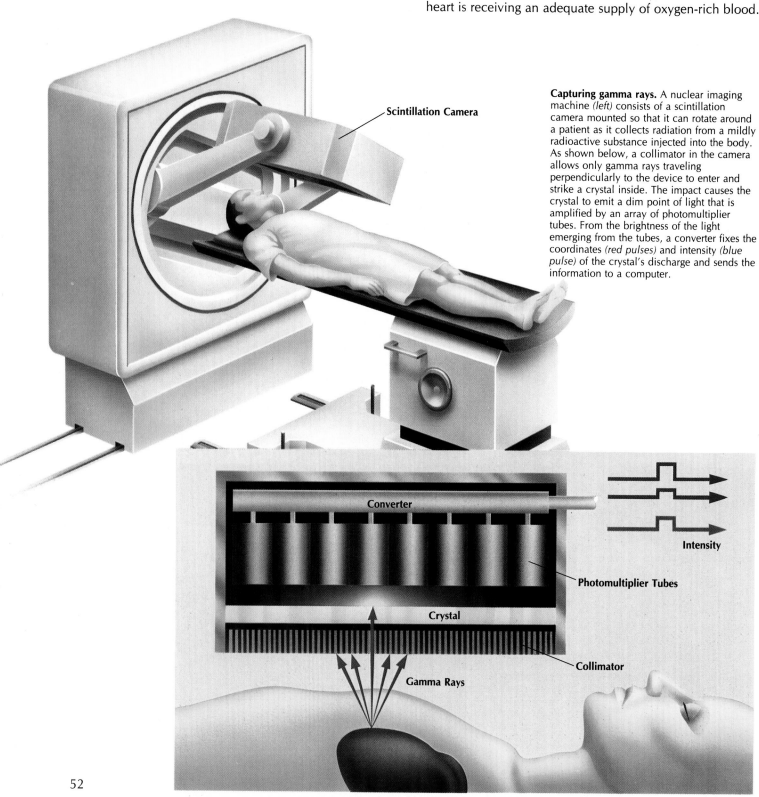

Capturing gamma rays. A nuclear imaging machine *(left)* consists of a scintillation camera mounted so that it can rotate around a patient as it collects radiation from a mildly radioactive substance injected into the body. As shown below, a collimator in the camera allows only gamma rays traveling perpendicularly to the device to enter and strike a crystal inside. The impact causes the crystal to emit a dim point of light that is amplified by an array of photomultiplier tubes. From the brightness of the light emerging from the tubes, a converter fixes the coordinates *(red pulses)* and intensity *(blue pulse)* of the crystal's discharge and sends the information to a computer.

Scintillation Camera

Converter

Intensity

Photomultiplier Tubes

Crystal

Collimator

Gamma Rays

As a first step in this investigative procedure, doctors inject radioactive thallium into the patient's bloodstream. The patient then exercises long enough for the chemical to collect in the heart muscle, and the radioactivity is measured. Several hours later, after blood coursing through the heart has had an opportunity to wash away most of the thallium, the radiation level is remeasured. How far it has fallen is an indication of the volume of blood reaching the heart: The weaker the residual radiation, the healthier the flow.

Detecting the infinitesimal amounts of radiation involved requires a device called a scintillation camera, explained at left. This sensitive instrument converts radiation, in the form of gamma rays, to electrical signals that are compiled by computer into images like the ones shown below.

Gamma-ray pictures. Nuclear images of a heart help doctors judge whether the organ's muscle tissue is getting enough blood through the coronary arteries. Both sets of images at right show three views of a heart, one from above and two from the left side. Comparing the top set with the adjacent color bar indicates that most of the radioactive thallium has been flushed from the muscle, a sign of unobstructed arteries and a healthy heart. Colors in the bottom set of images, however, fall at the unhealthy end of the color bar, indicating low blood flow and increased potential for a heart attack.

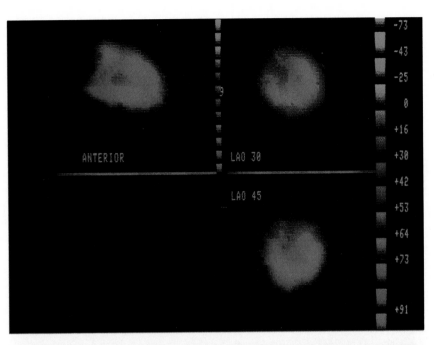

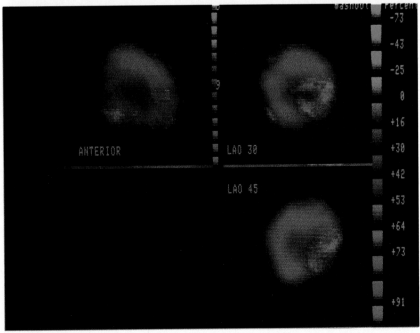

Echoes from Within

Ultrasonic imaging equipment uses high-frequency sound—two million hertz or higher—to produce images of internal organs. A series of short ultrasonic pulses from a device called a transducer penetrates the body. When a pulse encounters a boundary between two tissues of different densities—heart muscle and blood flowing through an artery, for example, or a fetus and the surrounding amniotic fluid in the womb—part of the sound energy is reflected to the transducer while the rest continues to the next tissue boundary. There another echo

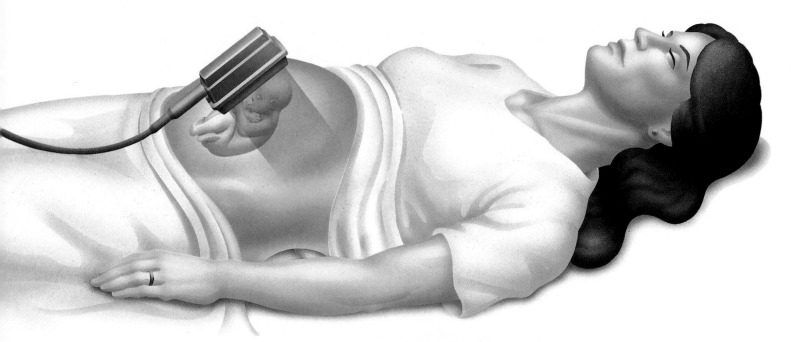

A string of reflections. The diagram at right shows the echoes from a pulse of ultrasonic sound as it passes from one type of tissue to another. Traveling from left to right, the pulse first encounters the boundary between layers of fat and muscle, a border that lets most of the pulse's sound energy pass. Even so, the echo produced there is strong because the pulse has as yet lost little energy. Echoes from the muscle-fluid and fluid-muscle boundaries are softer than the first echo, partly because the initial pulse has become weaker and partly because these borders also let pass most of the pulses' remaining sound energy. However, when the pulse strikes bone, which reflects almost all the residual energy, the echo is louder than all but the first one.

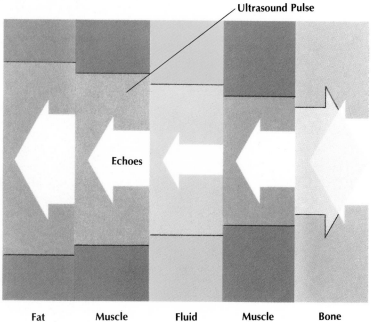

Ultrasound Pulse

Echoes

| Fat | Muscle | Fluid | Muscle | Bone |

occurs, and so on until the energy of the pulse is dissipated.

A computer analyzes thousands of such echoes from each pulse. Processing is complex, but in general, the time between a pulse going out and a reflection returning to the transducer is a measure of how far inside the body an echo originates. Reflections of equal strength are assigned one of a range of gray tones or colors. Combining the timing data with echo-strength information, the computer displays images like those of a fetus shown below. If the computer is also programmed to consider the frequency or pitch of the echoes that the transducer receives, ultrasound can reveal the flow of blood through veins and arteries *(bottom)*.

Ultrasound imaging is quick and easy, and it is thought to be much safer than x-ray techniques. A physician coats the skin with a special jelly, then holds the transducer against the patient. Instantly, a moving image appears on the monitor. The picture is especially useful for checking the development of a fetus, whose movements can be clues to its health.

Images of a fetus. These pictures indicate the clarity of detail doctors can obtain with ultrasound equipment. The image at right shows a clenched fist. At far right, facial features are clearly visible in an ultrasound picture made nineteen weeks into a pregnancy.

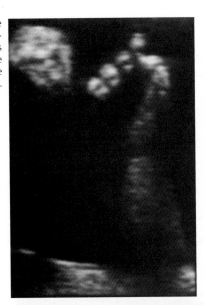
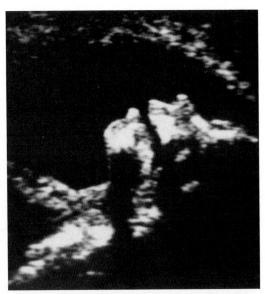

Currents in Conflict

The ability of ultrasound to reveal blood flow depends on the Doppler effect. Because of this phenomenon, the frequency of an echo returning from blood flowing away from the transducer is slightly lower than the frequency of the original pulse. Conversely, blood flowing toward the transducer produces an echo of slightly higher pitch. In this image of a carotid artery, blood flowing from right to left (toward the head and away from the transducer) is displayed in red, while blood flowing in the opposite direction is colored blue. As the heart beats, a strong eddy forms between two areas of plaque. Although the eddy appears to interrupt the flow of blood to the head, the blockage may be illusory, a product of fleeting turbulence as the blood pulses past the deposits of plaque.

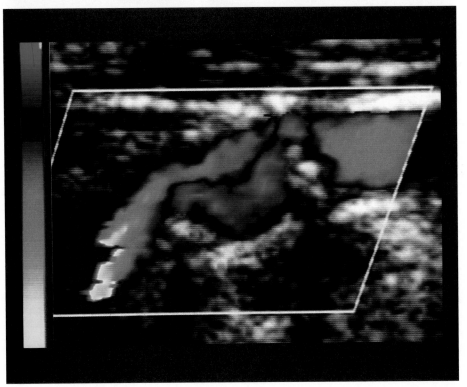

Pictures from Protons

Composed mostly of water, the human body contains an abundance of hydrogen atoms. As explained here, the application of a graduated magnetic field in concert with precisely tuned radio signals can influence these atoms to send out radio waves of their own. Tissues with a high water content, which have a comparatively large number of hydrogen atoms, emit stronger signals than tissues containing less water. This distinction can be used to produce finely detailed images, especially of the body's soft tissues.

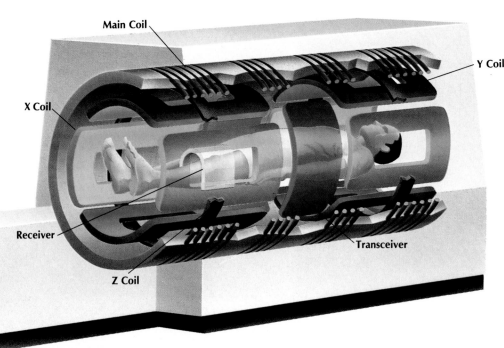

An MRI system consists of a tube girded by coils of powerful electromagnets. The main coil surrounds a patient with a uniform magnetic field. Three additional coils create magnetic gradients. X and Y coils produce gradients from left to right and top to bottom across the cylinder. The Z-coil gradient is stronger at one end of the tube than the other. Transceivers send radio signals to protons and receive signals from them. Special receivers are available to intercept signals from small parts of the body such as the knee (left).

X-coil slicing. To make a sagittal image with magnetic resonance, first a magnetic gradient from the X coils is applied to slice the patient sagittally (page 47). The resulting data is stored in the computer.

Y-coil slicing. Next, the sagittal slice is cut into strips using the magnetic field produced by the Y coils.

Z-coil slicing. Finally, each strip is cut into voxels by means of the magnetic gradient generated by the Z coils. From these voxels, the computer can display a view like the one at right.

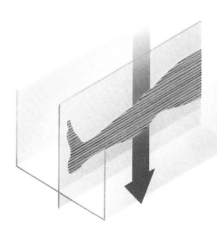
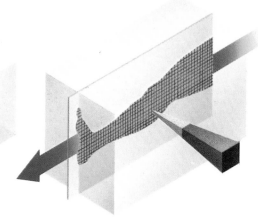

The principle behind this imaging technique is called magnetic resonance, meaning that the proton in a hydrogen nucleus spins with a wobble when placed under the influence of a magnetic field. A child's top, when it comes to a stop, wobbles in a similar manner just before falling on its side.

Called precession, the wobble makes the hydrogen atoms susceptible to radio energy of a specific frequency. Beamed into the body, the radio signal tilts the hydrogen atoms. When the signal is interrupted, the atoms return to their original positions, emitting a signal of the same frequency as they do so.

The exact frequency of the radio signal depends on the amount of precession, which in turn depends on the strengths of the magnetic fields. In practice, the fields are constructed as gradients—that is, stronger on one side than the other. Irradiating the body with a signal of a certain frequency confines the reaction of hydrogen nuclei to a thin slice of tissues. Diced into voxels, the slice can be processed by computer to yield images like the one at the bottom of this page.

  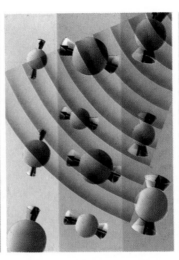 

Magnets off. In the absence of a magnetic gradient, the spin axes *(arrows)* of protons are randomly oriented. Here they are segregated into three separate areas that will become slices.

Magnets on. A magnetic gradient aligns the protons' spin axes and causes them to precess or wobble. Wobbling is least where the magnetic field is weakest *(above, left)*.

Signal on. Spin axes of protons in a single slice *(above, center)* tilt when struck by a radio signal tuned to the degree of wobble there. Protons in adjacent slices are unaffected.

Signal off. When the radio signal is turned off, the protons snap into realignment with the magnetic field. As they do so, the protons emit signals that a computer processes into an image.

A view of a knee. This magnetic resonance image, a sagittal slice through a knee, reveals a bright accumulation of blood behind the patient's kneecap.

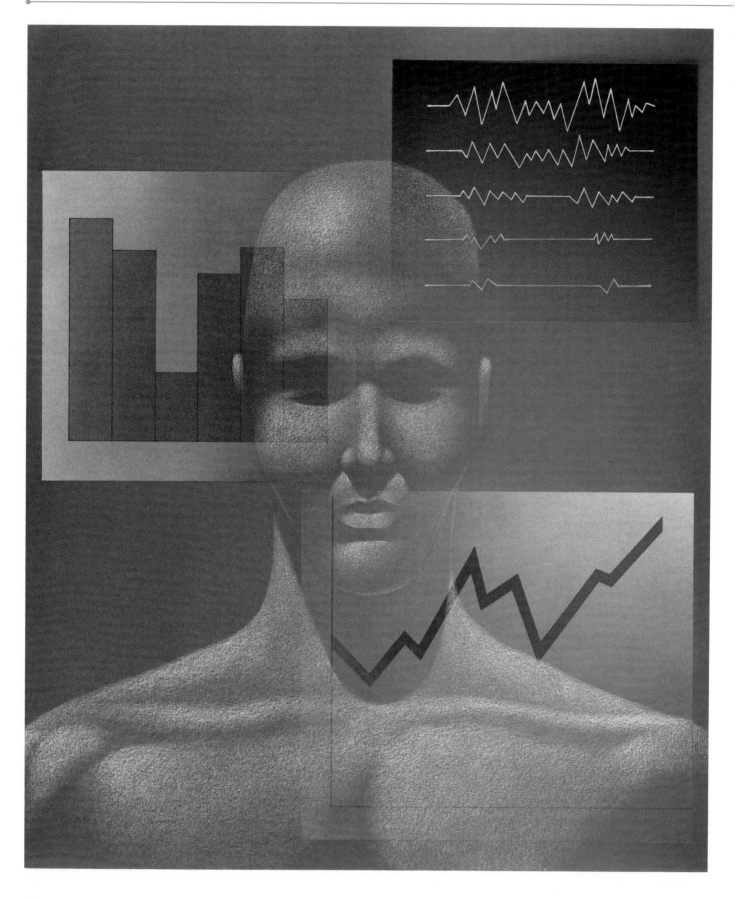

An Era of Automation

Modern medical practice is frequently described as an exercise in information management. Back in the nineteenth century, physicians struggled to cope with the stream of fresh facts flowing from medical laboratories. That stream was destined to develop into a flood. Seemingly familiar ailments suddenly became strangers. Cancer, for example, was found to be not one disease but many, each with different characteristics, treatments, and prognoses. Discovery upon discovery about the human body and its workings—or its failure to work correctly—tumbled into print.

Today, more than two million articles are published every year in the world's medical journals. Specialization has flourished, in part because it offers physicians a way to carve up and cope with the volumes of new knowledge. Certainly no general practitioner can keep pace with it; but even specialists are hard-pressed to stay up-to-date. Not surprisingly, doctors and hospitals have turned to computers for help.

In 1964, for example, a computer was put to work as medical assistant when *Index Medicus,* a venerable system for cataloging medical articles by subject, was converted into a database called the Medical Literature Analysis and Retrieval System, or MEDLARS. In 1971, MEDLARS became accessible via telephone and modem to computer terminals located anywhere in the world through a service called MEDLINE. Today, doctors have at their disposal the computerized cullings from 3,400 journals published throughout the world—some five million indexed citations in all, each summarized in a one-paragraph abstract. In the space of a few minutes, a physician can conduct a search that once would have required days or even weeks—and cover the subject more thoroughly than ever.

The amassing of bibliographic data is just one of many ways computers serve as information-management tools in the practice of medicine. Another important line of progress has been in the day-to-day care of hospital patients, which is dependent on the exchange of information between doctors, nurses, and laboratory specialists.

Two decades ago, information sclerosis afflicted even the best-run hospitals. Documents such as patient charts, laboratory tests, treatment orders, radiology and pathology reports, and prescriptions generated mounds of paper that consumed large amounts of space and—far worse—allowed abundant opportunity for error. Each patient had not a single record but many. A patient requiring laboratory tests, x-rays, and analysis of a biopsy would have separate records in three departments.

Results of the tests were sent to the nursing station, where they were noted on the patient's chart and filed until the doctor could examine them. Separate reports were sent to the accounting department, where clerks entered them one by one into the patient's billing record. The flow of information tended to be sluggish. Test results were usually delivered through the hospital's internal mail system; any greater speed required time-consuming telephone calls or costly special messengers.

In 1976, Boston's Beth Israel Hospital joined forces with the Harvard Medical School to create an electronic system that would end this informational nightmare. The result, completed after ten years of work, was a common registry of more than 500,000 patients—every one treated at Beth Israel since 1965, so that a number of returning patients would already be included. The registry is managed by a network of Data General Eclipse computers providing 12 billion characters of disk storage. Three hundred terminals provide immediate access to every record from stations throughout the hospital.

Beth Israel's patients enter the system when an admissions clerk logs them in and forwards their needs to the departments that will be responsible for their room assignments, meals, laundry, and mail delivery. A patient's arrival is also heralded by a printed message at the nursing station responsible for his or her room, and the data gathering continues as various tests are ordered and completed.

Many laboratory instruments automatically calculate test results; the laboratory's computers forward results to the central registry as soon as they are checked, making them im-

mediately available at any terminal in the hospital. Radiologists write their reports on word-processing terminals connected to the system so that these, too, can be reviewed immediately by nurses and attending physicians. In the pharmacy, the system compares each patient's prescriptions and issues a warning if it finds drugs that may create dangerous interactions. Naturally, the computer helps tend the books by automatically forwarding charges to the hospital's separate financial computer.

Although all information is available at all terminals throughout the hospital, access to the system is closely controlled in order to protect patient privacy. Each user is assigned a unique code that permits access only to information needed by that person, and only at certain designated terminals. Admissions clerks do not have access to laboratory-test results, for example, and their keys will not work at terminals outside the admitting department. Attending physicians, on the other hand, may obtain laboratory results, radiology reports, and other medical information at any terminal. Although it was long in the making, the system has proved a prodigious timesaver—dramatically improving the efficiency of doctors, nurses, and a number of other hospital professionals.

HELP ON THE WAY

At about the same time the Beth Israel network took shape, an even more ambitious information system was developed at Latter Day Saints Hospital in Salt Lake City, Utah. Its aim was not just to increase efficiency but also to "smooth the uneven quality" of hospital care, in the words of Dr. Homer Warner, chairman of the Latter Day Saints medical biophysics department, who directed the project. Warner had in mind a kind of electronic checklist for each patient that would remind doctors and nurses of the tests, medications, and other procedures ordinarily followed for a particular illness. The end product was a computerized system called HELP (for Health Evaluation through Logical Processing), which incorporates not only all patient records but also more than 3,000 items of information about medical practice at Latter Day Saints Hospital, including normal values for test results and information about drug interactions.

These stored items are called "rules." The computer is programmed to compare the data in each patient's record with appropriate rules and to issue an alert when it spots something abnormal—for example, a blood test that reveals an unusually low potassium level. HELP also reminds doctors and nurses to follow standard procedures. One procedure, for example, calls for patients to receive antibiotics a certain number of hours before surgery is to be performed; somewhat like a sophisticated alarm clock, HELP finds patients who are scheduled for surgery and tells doctors and nurses when the antibiotics are to be given. The result has been a marked decrease in the occurrence of infections following surgery.

Someday in the future, most big hospitals may have systems like HELP to regulate their internal workings. But because such computerization typically

Digital Subtraction Angiography

Angiography, a medical procedure in which an x-ray-absorbent chemical—usually iodine—is injected into blood vessels to make them stand out from other tissues, helps doctors to see veins and arteries that would be invisible in an x-ray made without the technique.

The procedure has its limitations. As shown in the angiograms below, the contrast between blood vessels and the tissue that surrounds them is slight at best, complicating diagnosis and treatment. However, a computer-age variation of the decades-old procedure, called digital subtraction angiog-

These x-rays of a hip joint show the difference in appearance between a typical reference x-ray (left) and an angiogram for DSA (right). Blood vessels invisible in the reference x-ray appear as dark shadows in the angiogram. A light patch at the top of the thighbone indicates the presence of a tumor, which x-rays pass through more readily than they do through healthy bone.

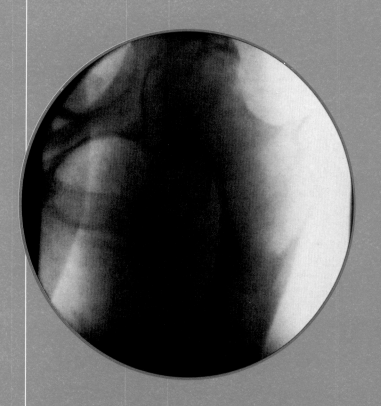
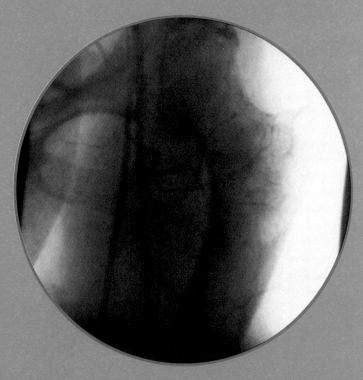

raphy (DSA), can make blood vessels stand out in stark relief.

DSA is as simple as comparing two x-rays. First, a reference x-ray is made without the dye. This image is then divided by computer into small squares called pixels, a process called digitizing. Each pixel is assigned numbers that stand for the amount of radiation absorbed by the tissue that each square represents. Next, iodine is injected into the blood. As the iodine-rich blood passes through the vessels under examination, a series of x-ray images is made, which the computer also digitizes.

Next, the computer compares pixel numbers of the reference x-ray to the numbers of corresponding pixels in the images produced from the iodine-infused blood. Where no iodine was present, the values are identical; the computer turns such pixels either black or white, depending on the wishes of the technologist operating the equipment. Pixels that remain are displayed in contrasting tones, resulting in a detailed image of blood flow through veins or arteries. Doctors can watch the process on a monitor as it happens, with as many as ten images being created each second.

In a DSA image based on the two x-rays at left, the shadowy arteries of the angiogram pop out of a white background. The large vessels running vertically are branches of the femoral artery. Smaller branches also feed the tumor, which appears as a gray smudge because of its rich supply of blood.

A third image shows the effectiveness of measures taken to stem the flow of blood to the tumor. Because doctors can see in the DSA image precisely which blood vessels are involved, they can inject a blocking agent into the vessels nourishing the abnormality before surgery to remove it. With the blood supply cut off, surgeons will encounter less bleeding as they cut out the tumor.

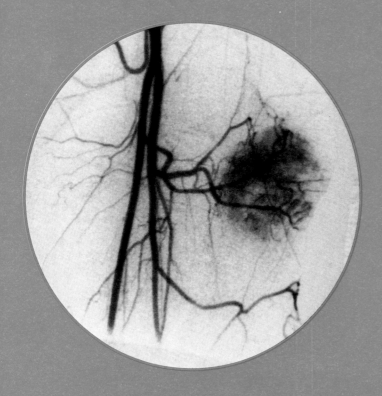 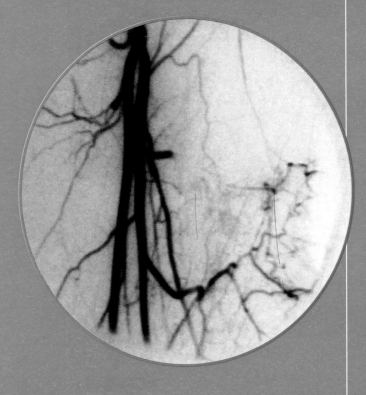

Measuring Bottlenecks

Detailed images of blood vessels provided by digital subtraction angiography are a great help to physicians in evaluating and treating vascular diseases such as atherosclerosis (hardening of the arteries). To reveal the damage caused by disease, a technologist first draws a line approximately along the center of the blood flow through a vessel in the digitized image. Working outward from the line along its entire length, the computer examines pixel values. An abrupt change between adjacent pixels indicates a boundary between iodine-

A DSA image of an obstructed artery *(right)* is analyzed by computer, yielding the display shown below. There, the image is enlarged and the boundaries of the artery outlined. Near the top of the screen appears a cross-sectional view of the artery with a vertical line near the left end at an open, healthy section. A similar line marks the blockage. The length of the artery segment is measured against the top or bottom edge of a graph, which also plots the narrowing and widening of the artery. The upper line shows diameter, read from the left edge of the graph; the lower line records area and is read from the right edge. As reported at the top of the display, the artery's diameter at the narrowest point is 71 percent smaller than the diameter of a healthy section. The area there is 92 percent smaller.

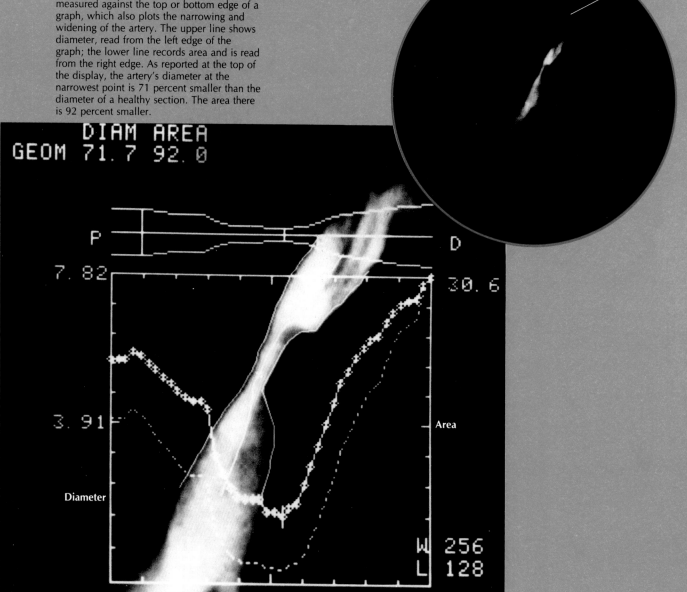

dyed blood and the undyed tissue of the blood-vessel wall.

To establish the scale of the image so that the computer can take accurate measurements, a technologist selects an object of known size within the image as a reference—often the catheter used to inject iodine into the patient. After comparing the actual size of the catheter to its image, the computer can deduce the blood vessel's diameter at dozens of points. The computer also calculates its cross-sectional area, a better measure of capacity than diameter.

As shown on these pages, DSA imagery can be used not only to see the extent of a blockage, but also as post-treatment procedure to observe whether a cure has succeeded. In this instance, the computerized angiograms show that, before treatment, cholesterol buildup had all but closed off a patient's iliac artery—a major blood vessel in the leg *(left)*. However, after the plaque deposits were removed by means of a tiny scraping device threaded into the artery, blood flow returned to normal *(below)*.

After removal of the blockage, the computer analysis shows that the artery has uniform diameter and area, with no significant peaks or valleys in the measurements. Indeed, the percentage difference between the healthy and formerly diseased sections of the blood vessel has declined to zero.

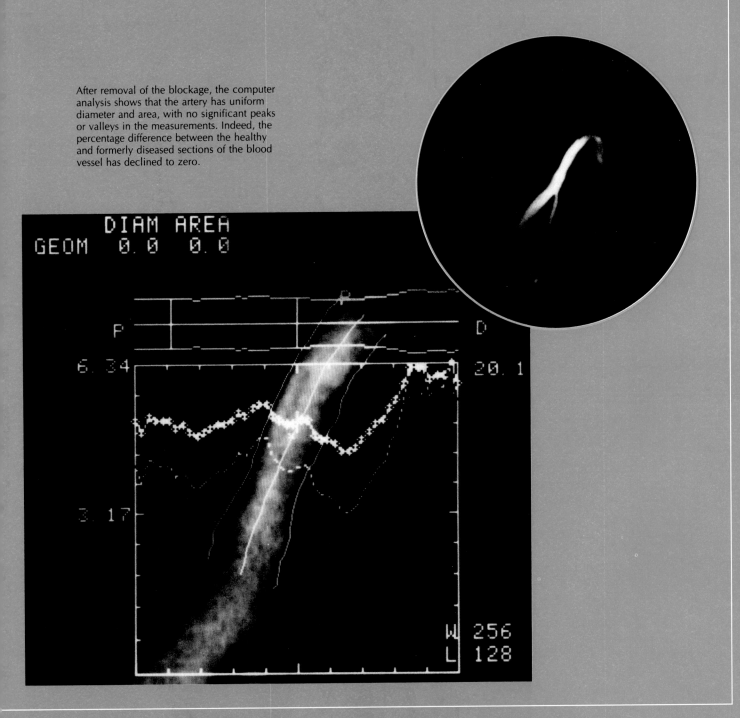

costs millions of dollars, that day will be slow in coming. The opposite is the case on another medical front—that of epidemiology. There, the conquest of the computer is complete.

MEDICAL DETECTIVES

Epidemiologists keep watch over the state of the public's health by tracking the spread of diseases, such as influenza or AIDS, and are called in from time to time to find the cause and cure of some particularly baffling outbreak of illness. Both as monitors and detectives, epidemiologists rely heavily on statistical analysis—the search, using mathematical techniques, for relationships between facts that can yield greater understanding of a disease, its origin, and the weapons that can be used to stop it. Mathematical models of communicable diseases enable health agencies to detect incipient epidemics, warn the public, and undertake preventive measures, such as immunization campaigns. Likewise, statistics are used at the scene of sudden, isolated disease outbreaks to help individual epidemiologists identify their cause. Today, when statistics are involved, so are computers.

The Centers for Disease Control—the United States' renowned epidemiological agency, located in Atlanta, Georgia—installed its first computer in 1966. This IBM 360 was employed to organize the mountains of data about disease that were sent to Atlanta weekly by state and municipal public-health officers. The reports detailed the number of cases of disease that occurred, and this information enabled the CDC to monitor changes that signaled problems or revealed the success or failure of preventive measures.

The computer's first job was to maintain the totals and retrieve them. More quickly than human mathematicians, it could provide the number of cases of a particular disease during the past month, or the number of cases reported in one state or another. As new computers were added (the CDC now uses a bank of high-speed IBM 3090 systems), statisticians were able to perform complex analyses in minutes.

But this speed was of little use to epidemiologists working in the field, attempting to isolate and stop the spread of a local outbreak of disease. Although statistics were no less important to them, they faced a processing bottleneck. Investigators conducted interviews, gathered records and other data, and returned to Atlanta, where they waited for programmers to design record formats, keypunchers to type in the information, supervisors to find and correct errors, and operators to run batches of data cards through the computer. Results were returned days or weeks after the data was turned in. A particularly tricky study could take months.

This began to change in the mid-1980s, as powerful personal computers appeared on the market and software especially designed for epidemiologists became available. CDC now has more than 1,500 microcomputers in its offices. Epidemiologists are trained in their use and routinely carry portable machines on their investigative forays.

INTENSIVE TROUBLE

A typical example of the portable computer's value occurred not long ago, in the case of an outbreak of blood infections among intensive-care patients in a

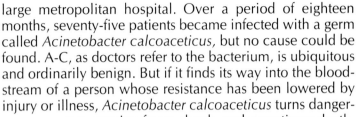

large metropolitan hospital. Over a period of eighteen months, seventy-five patients became infected with a germ called *Acinetobacter calcoaceticus,* but no cause could be found. A-C, as doctors refer to the bacterium, is ubiquitous and ordinarily benign. But if it finds its way into the bloodstream of a person whose resistance has been lowered by injury or illness, *Acinetobacter calcoaceticus* turns dangerous, causing fever, shock, and sometimes death. In fact, thirty of the patients who contracted the infection in this hospital had died from it. Hospital staff, municipal health officers, and epidemiologists from the state health department all tried to find the cause. Equipment was inspected, and doctors, nurses, and visitors were required to scrub and don sterile gowns. One unit of the hospital was closed to new admissions. Still, the infections continued.

Finally, the CDC was asked to help, and Dr. Consuelo Beck-Sagué, a pediatrician-turned-medical detective, was sent to the scene. Normally, Beck-Sagué spends her time examining reports from state and local public-health departments and conducting statistical studies that help pinpoint new concerns. (It was a routine study of this type by other epidemiologists at the Centers for Disease Control that first signaled the spread of AIDS in the early 1980s.) Three or four times a year, Beck-Sagué is called away from her office in Atlanta to work on particularly vexing outbreaks. Her constant companion on these trips is a Compaq portable computer.

Beck-Sagué put her computer to work on the case even before leaving CDC. With a modem, she used it to search MEDLINE, where she found a score of articles describing the infections that attack patients in intensive-care units, the equipment used in such units, and *Acinetobacter calcoaceticus* itself. This research led her to suspect that some piece of medical paraphernalia was introducing the germ directly into the patients' blood.

After she had met with the hospital staff and heard their theories, Beck-Sagué started what is known as a case-control study—a comparison of cases (intensive-care-unit patients who contracted the infection) with controls (patients who did not). The aim was to find, among the many similarities between the two groups, the crucial, hidden differences, known as risk factors, that would point to the cause. To be successful, the study had to compare data for as many patients as possible—and the data had to include every possible risk factor.

Beck-Sagué selected 109 patients for her study. From their records she extracted more than 100 factors that could be directly compared. Those factors included each patient's age and other demographic information, the type of underlying illness or injury and its severity, the length of hospital stay, the days on which patients contracted the infection, their medications, and the equipment used in treating and monitoring them, such as respirators, catheters, and sensors that transmit data about blood pressure, pulse, and other vital signs to the ICU computers. The complete study would gather and analyze more than 10,000 items of information.

A SKEPTICAL STAFF

Despite Beck-Sagué's methodical approach, the hospital staff was prepared to be wary of her answers. This problem had defied them for nearly eighteen months; how could she solve it in a few days?

The answer lay in the array of talents CDC requires of its epidemiologists. They must be skilled bacteriologists who can quickly and accurately find and identify disease organisms, careful clinicians who can recognize and interpret symptoms and develop strategies for treatment, and trained statisticians who can digest and analyze volumes of data.

Beck-Sagué's indispensable weapon was a program called Epi Info, designed for tasks just such as this. Epi Info was born as one segment of a much larger program dreamed up by Dr. Andrew Dean, a former Minnesota State Epidemiologist and a veteran of epidemic investigations in the United States, Africa, and the Pacific. Dean had long wanted to provide epidemiologists in the field with the data-gathering and statistical processing powers that existed at the home office. He recognized the possibilities presented by the microcomputers introduced in the early 1980s, and he set to work developing nothing less than an office-in-a-box—a word processor, communications terminal, data-gathering program, and statistical analyst. He called this software edifice Epi Aid, and it was successful—sort of. "The program worked, but it was hardly 'user friendly,' " Dean recalls.

The most satisfactory portion of the package was Epi Info—the data-gathering and analysis segment of Epi Aid. It was the product of a four-way collaboration of Andrew Dean, CDC systems analyst Tony Burton, epidemiologist and statistician Dr. Richard Dicker, and Dean's son, Jeff, who started writing the program in the programming language Pascal when he was a high-school student working as an intern at CDC.

Epi Info helps manage the huge volume of data that is both bread and butter and bane of an epidemiologist's existence. At heart, it is a database program. It enables the investigator to create a questionnaire on the computer screen that can be printed, copied, and used by interviewers. The computerized questionnaire also serves as an entry form for the database, automatically formatting information and checking for errors. Finally, Epi Info runs the statistical analyses that are used to link disease with risk factors, and it makes the results available immediately. The program even creates charts and graphs to help explain and persuade.

A CLUE EMERGES

Beck-Sagué enlisted the help of a state epidemiologist and the doctor and nurse in charge of the hospital's infection-control measures to copy information from patients' charts into Epi Info's database. The work was tedious, requiring more than an hour to extract the necessary data from each patient's files. On the third day, with just twenty cases and twenty controls entered, the researchers could wait no longer to find out if the data revealed any clues. "That's the beauty of the computer," Beck-Sagué says. "You can stop at any time, run an analysis, and see what you've got."

What they had was a clue: Into the artery of each infected patient a tiny catheter had been inserted and connected to a sensor that provided a continuous blood-pressure reading. Somehow, when the catheter went into the patient's artery, the *Acinetobacter calcoaceticus* organism went with it. The statistics revealed that patients with these devices were eight to nine times more likely to be infected with A-C than those without them. The hospital staff was incredulous. They demanded proof.

As it turned out, the problem lay with a protective device built into the instrument. The workings of the catheter were simple. When it was inserted into the artery, the patient's blood rose in a small tube. Sterile water in the top of the tube served as a buffer between the blood and the tube's cap, which incorporated the sensor—a transducer that converted the fluid's pressure into an electrical signal that was sent to the intensive-care unit's computer. The cap was fitted with a disposable membrane to protect the patient's bloodstream from the rest of the mechanism and from outside germs. The membrane was also intended to eliminate the need to sterilize the delicate transducers. Since the membrane was discarded after every use, it seemed unlikely that infection could pass from sensor to blood—or so the hospital staff believed.

Nonetheless, Epi Info's rapid return of statistical evidence persuaded officials to examine the suspect instruments closely. Soon, bacterial cultures confirmed that the devices were, indeed, to blame. The *Acinetobacter calcoaceticus* bacteria, allowed to collect on the unsterilized transducer, easily made their way onto the surface of the membrane as the instrument was being assembled. From there, the bacteria went directly into the patient's bloodstream. When the transducers themselves were sterilized, the infection disappeared. In a few days, Consuelo Beck-Sagué and her computer had isolated and removed the cause of the deadly infection.

FORECASTING AN EPIDEMIC

By the late 1980s, more than 3,000 copies of Epi Info had been distributed by Dean and his colleagues to public-health agencies and universities. Microcomputers do not eliminate epidemiologists' need for powerful mainframe machines, however. These are still used to maintain, collect, and organize data and to perform ever-more-sophisticated statistical analyses, such as the prediction of a disease's spread.

More than two decades ago, influenza was targeted for forecasting of this kind. Few diseases are more routinely destructive. An estimated 20 million people died in the worldwide epidemic of 1918-1919, and in nearly every decade the virus gains a foothold in one city, then leapfrogs around the world, following the path of travelers as they move from nation to nation. Even the mildest outbreaks of the disease cost thousands of lives and billions of dollars in lost wages and medical expenses.

The first program to predict an influenza epidemic's spread was developed in the Soviet Union by Dr. Leonid A. Rvachev and Dr. Oganes Vagarshakovitch Baroyan. Their approach to the problem was simple. They knew that influenza was transmitted by close contact between people. They knew that the disease has an incubation period of about three days, and that during this time it can be transmitted to others.

They knew, too, that some people are immune to the virus and that the number of these people can be calculated from data gathered in the first days of an outbreak. So can the disease's "basic reproductive rate"—the average number of additional people each victim will infect. A rate of one means that the disease will be self-sustaining: that is, each sick person will pass on the ailment to one other before he or she gets well. If the basic reproductive rate is less than one, the disease will fade away. As the rate rises above one, the severity of an epidemic increases.

An opportunity for Rvachev and Baroyan to test the efficacy of their forecasting program presented itself in 1968 and 1969, during the now-infamous Hong Kong flu epidemic, named after the city where it emerged. The Soviet computers analyzed Hong Kong influenza cases reported during a three-week period in July 1968 and discovered that the basic reproductive rate of the flu strain was 1.89. This meant that the number of victims would nearly double every three days. A serious epidemic was at hand.

To learn where and when the flu would spread, the scientists created a mathematical description of travel among the fifty-two largest cities of the world, obtaining the raw data from international air-transport records. The result:

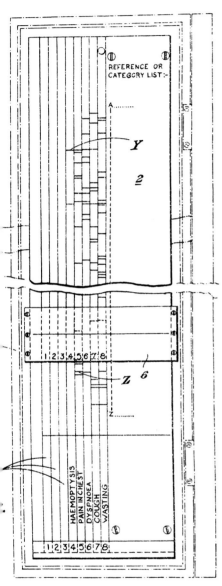

Within the figure:

REFERENCE OR
CATEGORY LIST:-

A.........

Y

2

| 1 2 3 4 5 6 7 8 |

Z *6*

Z.........

HAEMOPTYSIS
PAIN IN CHEST
DYSPNOEA
COUGH
WASTING

| 1 2 3 4 5 6 7 8 |

British physician Firmin A. Nash included this drawing of his diagnostic slide rule in a patent application filed on December 20, 1954. To use the slide rule, shown here standing on end, a doctor inserted strips of wood representing as many as eight symptoms observed in a patient. Marks on the strips aligned with diseases, printed in an alphabetical Reference or Category List, that might produce each symptom. A disease having several symptoms associated with it, as at Y in the diagram, was the likely diagnosis.

They predicted the arrival of the epidemic within a few days in all but three cities. That forecast required more than 16 million computations. Since this successful debut, the program has been improved and expanded to include more than 200 cities—a forecast that involves hundreds of millions of calculations. It is used by many national health agencies, including the United States' own Centers for Disease Control.

A DEADLIER PUZZLE

Despite their success in predicting the behavior of influenza, epidemiologists have found that other life-threatening diseases are not so easily modeled. Acquired immune deficiency syndrome, or AIDS, became their target in the 1980s, but even the application of the supercomputer resources of the United States, West Germany, and Great Britain has failed to produce a forecast of the course of that dreaded disease.

The sticking point is not computational but informational; there are too many variables, many of them introduced by the disease's long incubation period—five to ten years. During this time, the victim's ability to transmit the disease fluctuates and interacts with the dozens of other factors that influence the spread of AIDS, such as the number of sexual contacts. The result is a web of poorly understood relationships that must nevertheless be given a mathematical description by would-be AIDS modelers.

DIGITAL DIAGNOSIS

Spread of disease, though fascinating to most doctors, is the business of relatively few of them. Most physicians are concerned chiefly with diagnosis and treatment of their patients' ills. Today, the flow of information to doctors has increased both the expectation and the possibility of precise diagnosis; however, finding pertinent data in the stream is difficult, even with the help of computer data banks such as MEDLINE.

Doctors have been looking for ways to slash through the diagnostic thickets for decades. In 1954, a British physician, Firmin A. Nash, developed a diagnostic "fact manipulator" that enabled him to match symptoms with more than 300 diseases. Nash called his brainchild a "slide rule" because it looked like an overgrown version of the then-indispensable engineers' calculator. A list of diseases was printed from top to bottom, down the right side of the device. To the left of the list of diseases was a space into which as many as eight strips of wood were placed vertically. Each of the strips represented a symptom, and each was scribed with a number of horizontal lines pointing to diseases associated with that symptom.

A diagnosis could not be made with just one strip. When multiple strips were inserted into their space, the doctor would usually find that three, four, or more lines were aligned opposite a single disease. That ailment was therefore considered the most probable diagnosis. The device was large and unwieldy, but it was a successful attempt to codify the information a doctor used to narrow difficult diagnostic choices. Had the computer age not overtaken the invention, Nash's slide rule might have become a commonplace piece of equipment in physicians' offices.

Yet another system of mechanized diagnosis was tried in 1958, when physicians at the Cornell Medical Center in New York and the University of Pennsylvania in Philadelphia put a card sorter to work on the problem of diagnosing blood disorders. These present a particularly tough challenge to diagnosticians because different blood ailments, requiring quite different treatments, can often be distinguished only by subtle differences in symptoms or test data. The researchers hoped that mechanical sorting could cut through the tangle of complex diagnostic data.

Their method required no extraordinary equipment. The principal tool was a set of twenty-six standard eight-by-ten-inch data cards, one for each major blood disease. Around the edge of each card were 138 numbered notches and holes representing symptoms; a notch meant that disease was accompanied by that particular symptom, a hole meant it was not. To conduct a simple sort—to see what blood diseases were characterized by an enlarged spleen, for example—the cards were lined up front to back, and a metal or plastic rod was inserted into the space representing "enlarged spleen." When the rod was raised, the cards for diseases that were linked to an enlarged spleen would remain in place; those with holes (representing a normal spleen) were lifted out. To achieve a diagnosis, the process was repeated until all of a patient's symptoms had been tested against the cards.

On the first attempt, the doctors sorted the symptoms of eighty patients—symptom by symptom, patient by patient—and correctly identified the ailments of seventy-three of them. In fifty of the cases, a single card remained at the end of the sort—every one a correct diagnosis. In twenty-three of the cases, more than one card remained, requiring doctors to examine the symptoms more closely to see which pointed most strongly to a final diagnosis. In the seven remaining cases, for which no cards remained in place, they found that multiple ailments had, in effect, confused the system and forced it to yield no diagnosis. The experiment was deemed a success, and it encouraged the computer experiments that were to follow.

IF-THEN WHAT?

The card-sorting experiment used mechanical means to approximate diagnostic computing's classic conditional statement: "IF this symptom is present, THEN that disease should be considered." The card sorter did so by inverting the process: "IF this patient does not have this symptom, THEN that diagnosis should be rejected." With the advent of electronic computers, doctors were able to apply statistical techniques to calculate the probability of each diagnosis by weighting symptoms and disease characteristics—crudely emulating the thought process of the human diagnostician.

As they fashioned faster, more complex diagnostic programs, researchers began exploring the possibility that computers could not only suggest a diagnosis but recommend treatment as well. Among the pioneers in this effort were Dr. Edward Shortliffe, Edward Feigenbaum, and Bruce Buchanan of Stanford University. In the early 1970s, they produced a program called MYCIN, which took its name from the ending of the names of many antibiotics. MYCIN started where the Cornell/Penn card sorter of 1958 left off; after MYCIN diagnosed a blood infection, it then matched the diagnosis with recommended antibiotic therapies. A decade later, Shortliffe and Stanford's Lawrence Fagan created ONCOCIN, which helps doctors manage the complexities of chemotherapy for some types of cancer *(pages 79-87)*.

From the standpoint of the average physician, these programs were not much more than interesting curiosities, relevant to the needs of a few medical specialists. It remained to be seen whether computerized diagnosis of a broad range of illnesses was possible—and whether it was something doctors wanted. A wealth of research has given an affirmative answer to the first question. The jury is out on the second.

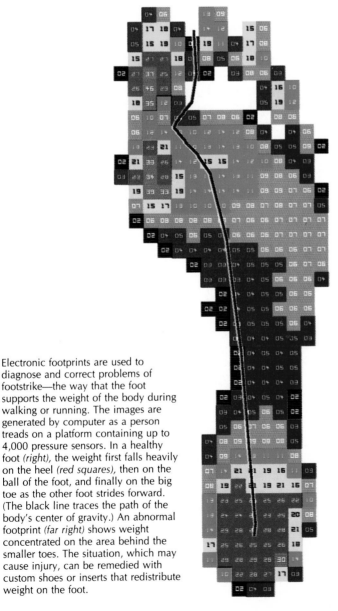

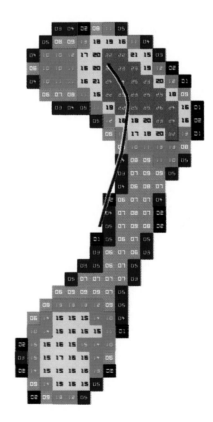

Electronic footprints are used to diagnose and correct problems of footstrike—the way that the foot supports the weight of the body during walking or running. The images are generated by computer as a person treads on a platform containing up to 4,000 pressure sensors. In a healthy foot *(right)*, the weight first falls heavily on the heel *(red squares)*, then on the ball of the foot, and finally on the big toe as the other foot strides forward. (The black line traces the path of the body's center of gravity.) An abnormal footprint *(far right)* shows weight concentrated on the area behind the smaller toes. The situation, which may cause injury, can be remedied with custom shoes or inserts that redistribute weight on the foot.

One of the first broad-based diagnostic programs was Internist-1, a system that was developed in the early 1970s at the University of Pittsburgh by Harry Pople, a computer scientist, and Dr. Jack Meyers, a professor of internal medicine.

The aim of Internist-1 was to incorporate the knowledge necessary to diagnose more than 700 diseases. Even in advanced editions, this goal was never quite met. When work stopped on the program in 1980, it could handle 5,000 variations on 650 diseases. The scope of the program is nonetheless impressive. A microcomputer version called QMR, or Quick Medical Reference, includes information about 577 diseases and their relationships. This program not only supplies diagnoses based on information provided by the physician—symptoms and test results, for example—but also asks the doctor for more information when it is needed. Furthermore, the program permits physicians to conduct "what-if" analyses by adding or subtracting symptoms to see if and how a diagnosis would change. Internist-1 and its offspring are at least as good at their job as the typical general practitioner.

DECISIONS DXPLAINED

Most physicians are still uncomfortable with the notion of computer diagnosis, and programs such as QMR and ONCOCIN have not yet found their way into widespread use. A diagnostic tool introduced in 1987 attempts to win over doctors in a way suggested by its name, DXplain. Since doctors are not inclined to take a computer's opinion at face value, this program explains its decisions. (The DX in the name is the medical shorthand for diagnosis.) The program was produced by the American Medical Association and a team from the Laboratory of Computer Science of Massachusetts General Hospital and Harvard Medical School. DXplain can be used by any doctor who has a computer, a telephone, and a modem: The doctor simply has to dial AMA/NET, which is the American Medical Association's on-line network. The program is based on a familiar information source, the association's publication *Current Medical Information and Terminology (CMIT)*, which summarizes symptoms, laboratory findings, and many other signs for more than 3,000 different illnesses. Out of these, DXplain's creators culled 2,000 diseases and

4,700 symptoms whose relationships were painstakingly weighed and measured. In all, the program includes some 65,000 linkages among various diseases and their symptoms.

When a doctor logs in to DXplain, the system asks for personal data about the patient, such as age, sex, and weight, then goes on to request symptoms and the results of laboratory tests. Possible diagnoses are displayed on the screen in the order of their probability, and they are explained by listing the symptoms supporting them.

The program also lists symptoms that the doctor did not report—a reminder to the physician of examinations or tests that may have been overlooked. Doctors also can talk back to the machine; they can interrupt the process at any time to send comments or questions via an electronic mailbox that is built into the system. The comments provide a stream of expert advice that can be used to improve the program.

CHARTING MENTAL ILLNESS

The application of computers to the treatment of mental illness and neurological disorders has lagged far behind their application to physical ailments. The first appearance of computers in this field, in 1966, was accidental—the consequence of an experiment in artificial-intelligence programming by Joseph Weizenbaum, a computer scientist at the Massachusetts Institute of Technology. In effect, Weizenbaum created a computer confidant.

Its name was Eliza, after Eliza Doolittle, the character in George Bernard Shaw's play *Pygmalion* and the musical comedy *My Fair Lady*. Weizenbaum chose the name because his Eliza, he explained, "could be taught to speak increasingly well, although it was never quite clear whether or not, like Miss Doolittle, she became smarter."

The computerized Eliza took her cues not from Professor Higgins, but from a famous American psychotherapist, Carl Rogers, a proponent of a technique called nondirective therapy. Instead of guiding his patients, Rogers reflected their statements back to them. The statement "Doctor, I'm not feeling good" would earn the response, "So, you're not feeling good?" rather than, "Where does it hurt?" This approach, said Rogers, forced the patient to engage in self-examination and led to greater understanding.

Weizenbaum's experiment was successful at demonstrating both the strengths and weaknesses of computerized "thinking." A conversation with Eliza could be cryptic, as this exchange with a magazine writer demonstrates:

Writer: How old are you?
Eliza: What answer would please you most?
Writer: The correct one.
Eliza: What does that suggest to you?
Writer: That I am a journalist. Just answer the question.
Eliza: Do you believe it normal to be a journalist?
Writer: I wouldn't call it normal, no. But it is my job.
Eliza: That's quite interesting.

Weizenbaum put Eliza in the public domain to encourage wide use and comment, and the program soon attracted attention outside the field of computer science. Despite Eliza's obvious limitations, mental health professionals adopted

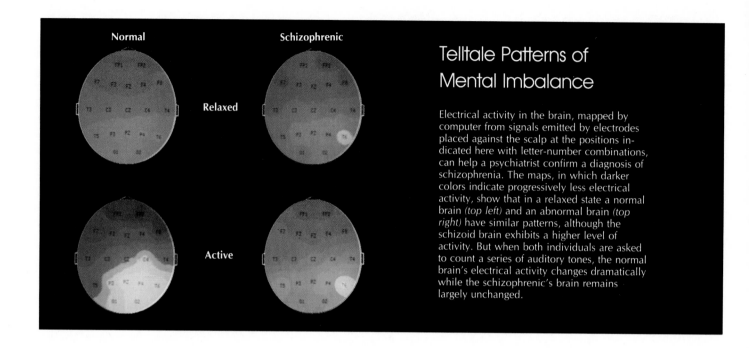

Telltale Patterns of Mental Imbalance

Electrical activity in the brain, mapped by computer from signals emitted by electrodes placed against the scalp at the positions indicated here with letter-number combinations, can help a psychiatrist confirm a diagnosis of schizophrenia. The maps, in which darker colors indicate progressively less electrical activity, show that in a relaxed state a normal brain *(top left)* and an abnormal brain *(top right)* have similar patterns, although the schizoid brain exhibits a higher level of activity. But when both individuals are asked to count a series of auditory tones, the normal brain's electrical activity changes dramatically while the schizophrenic's brain remains largely unchanged.

many of the program's features for software of their own. Computer programs have since proved to be an effective means of taking patient histories and helping to counsel students in their career choices.

However, less reputable practitioners have also been known to sell "therapy" sessions with Eliza to gullible clients. Weizenbaum was appalled by such abuses, and he disowned the creature in his book *Computer Power and Human Reason* in 1976. Nevertheless, Eliza continues to entertain and enlighten home computer users to this day.

THE COMPUTER AND THE EEG

A totally different way of using computers in the field of mental health has its roots in work begun in 1977 by a team of researchers led by Dr. E. Roy John of New York University. They compiled and analyzed electroencephalograms (EEGs) taken from more than 5,000 children and adults, each of whom had undergone other neurological and psychiatric examinations and had been judged either "normal" or suffering from a mental illness or a brain dysfunction such as a learning disorder.

EEGs measure electrical activity in the brain by recording—on paper or on a computer disk—the signals received by twenty-one electrodes placed against the patient's scalp. Because the number of electrodes and their position are determined by an international standard system, EEG data taken from many patients can be compared.

Statistical analysis of the EEGs showed the researchers that electrical activity in the brains of normal subjects differed noticeably from that of people who were mentally ill or had brain dysfunctions. They also found that each mental illness or dysfunction had its own characteristic electrical pattern. Disorders covered by the study included two types of depression, dementia caused by strokes, senile dementia, Alzheimer's disease, schizophrenia, brain damage from alcoholism or head injury, and six types of learning disabilities.

This was just the kind of information that a properly programmed and equipped computer could use to help psychiatrists and neurologists. Accurate diagnosis is always important, but it became even more so in the 1970s as potent new drugs were developed for the treatment of various mental illnesses. Because the drugs could have severe side effects, making a correct diagnosis was more critical than ever.

A COMPACT SPECTRUM

About the time E. Roy John was beginning his research at New York University, Carlton Cadwell, a dentist, and his brother John, a physician and electrical engineer, were founding Cadwell Laboratories, Inc., in Kennewick, Washington. Their company built computer-based electronic monitors and diagnostic instruments that test the health of nerves and muscles by measuring the electrical activity in them. Thus, it was not difficult for the Cadwells to understand how they might construct an instrument that would put the N.Y.U. research to work in doctors' offices.

In early 1987, after two years' development, the Spectrum 32 emerged from Cadwell Laboratories. Described by the company as a "neurometric analyzer," the machine is a 320-pound, four-foot-high cabinet fitted with four computers, two printers, a high-resolution graphics monitor, and an optical disk that is capable of storing 2,300 megabytes of data accumulated from a patient's EEGs. The Spectrum uses an IBM-AT personal computer, keyboard, and mouse to control three Motorola 68010 microprocessors—relatives of the popular 68000 found in the Apple Macintosh. Each of these microprocessors is assigned a single task: One acquires and processes information, one generates high-resolution color graphics for display on the color monitor, and the third manages the flow of data.

Although the machine is intended primarily to guide a psychiatric diagnosis, it may also be fitted with options to monitor the flow of oxygen to the brain during heart surgery, measure responses to a number of visual and acoustic signals, and—paired with a video camera—simultaneously record the activities and brain functions of a sleeping patient.

The Spectrum's neurometric analysis begins—like a stereotypical Freudian analysis—with the patient seated in a dimly lighted room. But there the similarity to tradition stops. The patient wears what looks like an antique cloth aviator's helmet, which contains the EEG sensors and holds them tight to the patient's head. While the subject sits quietly, with eyes closed, the instrument records signals from the brain, requiring about fifteen minutes to gather enough information for analysis.

Later, the doctor displays the data on the machine's monitor—twenty-one irregular lines moving across the screen—and uses its analysis of the tracings to extract two minutes of "artifact-free" readings (data containing no irregularities). These "artifacts" are caused by patient movement or reaction to outside noises—even the blink of an eye. The Spectrum automatically converts the EEG signals into a stream of numbers and runs a series of statistical tests so that the patient's results can be compared with those in the database. Nearly 400 characteristics of the patient's EEG, ranging from its strength to the coordination of signals, are matched against those stored in the system.

The results are displayed on the computer screen in a brief report that tells the doctor the probability of the patient suffering from a disorder covered by the research. The doctor can then print the report, analyze and print the data, and even produce colored brain maps that graphically compare the patient's EEG readings with those of other people, normal and abnormal.

Carlton Cadwell carefully points out that the Spectrum is an aid to diagnosis that "provides statistical comparisons of patient data with certain other populations"—the healthy and ill subjects of E. Roy John's studies. "These should be used in conjunction with other findings," he says. Nevertheless, Cadwell says he answers a steady stream of calls from doctors and others looking for a doc-in-a-box. "This isn't it," he tells them.

A WIDER ROLE

No one seriously expects computers to replace physicians. Time and again, computer programs have demonstrated that they can diagnose illness about as well as the average practitioner, but they are a far cry from the thoughtful, resourceful, imaginative, caring doctor most people want to treat them. Computerized information systems for hospitals have demonstrated great promise, but because such systems are very complex and extremely costly, progress on that front has been slow. Yet the practice of medicine depends on timely, up-to-date, detailed knowledge in a way that few other professions do. There can be little doubt that computers, being consummate knowledge machines, will play an ever-widening role.

Medical Experts on Line

The practice of medicine has long required mastery of vast quantities of information. New research is continually adding to the supply—and in the process, threatening to overwhelm individual physicians seeking to provide the best possible care for their patients. Computers, in addition to their many other contributions to the field, are now helping doctors take better advantage of these informational riches.

The assistance in this case comes in the form of expert systems, computer programs that combine extensive data on a particular subject with procedures that, in effect, simulate the reasoning powers of an expert. In medicine, such systems serve as electronic specialists, guiding physicians toward correct diagnoses or courses of treatment by supplying in-depth information and calling attention to details and possibilities that might otherwise be overlooked. Although they cannot match the on-the-spot counsel of human specialists, these systems aim to supply a useful measure of expertise by responding to a physician's questions and statements much as an advising colleague would.

Because of the processing power and memory capacity they require, most medical expert systems reside in minicomputers, but they are readily accessible on personal computers or desktop work stations through modem and network connections. Designed to incorporate new data easily, they offer the potential of enabling rural doctors and small local hospitals to benefit almost instantaneously from the front-line research of big-city medical centers.

Expert systems follow the same tendency as doctors to specialize. Using the case of a hypothetical patient, the following pages present simplified versions of three actual systems developed at medical centers in the United States: DXplain *(pages 82-83)*, a diagnostic aid developed at Massachusetts General Hospital; the University of Southern California's Intellipath, used in pathology for identifying tissue specimens *(pages 84-85)*; and ONCOCIN, created at Stanford University for charting and managing the course of cancer treatments *(pages 86-87)*.

Building on a Base of Knowledge

Although medical expert systems differ in specifics depending on the areas of medicine they were tailored for, all share common design features. The foundation is always information—an enormous amount of it, representing expert knowledge on a given subject. To turn this into a so-called knowledge base that a computer can manipulate, a specialized programmer dubbed a knowledge engineer translates the statements of experts into a form the computer can understand—very commonly, if-then rules. Such rules establish firm links between facts and conclusions for the computer to

Converting knowledge. The statements and arrows below represent how a knowledge engineer establishes a knowledge base by transforming medical data into a language of if-then rules that organizes the information for the computer. In the first example, a simple statement of mononucleosis symptoms is rendered into three conditions or premises and a single conclusion. The use of basic mathematical symbols and clearly defined terms and punctuation (a comma means *and*) facilitates the further translation into computer code.

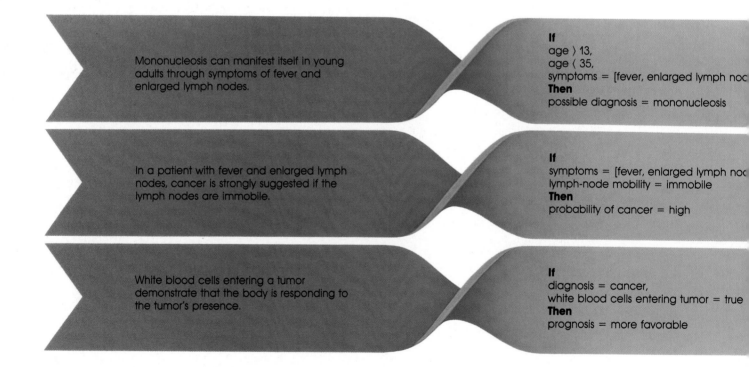

Mononucleosis can manifest itself in young adults through symptoms of fever and enlarged lymph nodes.

If
age ⟩ 13,
age ⟨ 35,
symptoms = [fever, enlarged lymph nod
Then
possible diagnosis = mononucleosis

In a patient with fever and enlarged lymph nodes, cancer is strongly suggested if the lymph nodes are immobile.

If
symptoms = [fever, enlarged lymph nod
lymph-node mobility = immobile
Then
probability of cancer = high

White blood cells entering a tumor demonstrate that the body is responding to the tumor's presence.

If
diagnosis = cancer,
white blood cells entering tumor = true
Then
prognosis = more favorable

follow, with due allowance for the uncertainties inherent in many medical judgments.

Computers are, of course, relentlessly literal, and a good knowledge engineer must work closely with experts to achieve a satisfactory conceptualization of their reasoning and methods. The specific computer procedures for manipulating the knowledge base are embodied in a separate part of the program known as the inference engine. Its carefully delineated ability to make connections enables an expert system, for example, to reason forward from a symptom to a disease or backward from a disease to a symptom. Because it is technically separate, the inference engine is unaffected by the addition or changing of information in the knowledge base; the same rules of reasoning apply no matter what the specifics of the data being processed.

A "doctor-friendly" interface is an important part of any system. In some designs, the program presents a menu and the doctor selects entries with a mouse. Other expert systems use subroutines to translate a doctor's own typed-in words into the program's controlled list of terms.

Extracting advice. When a doctor queries an expert system, the part of the program known as the inference engine goes into effect, drawing conclusions by making connections between pieces of information within the organized structure of the knowledge base. This sort of programming must be flexible enough to guide a physician to whatever information might be relevant, no matter how obscure.

Help from a Digital Diagnostician

A young man who has not been feeling well for several weeks finally makes an appointment to see his physician. His symptoms could betoken any of several different diseases, from the benign to the deadly. The doctor faces two immediate challenges: to generate a list of diseases broad enough to include all reasonable possibilities, and to narrow that list as quickly as possible so that proper treatment can begin.

Medical expert systems geared to the diagnostic phase have the informational and processing resources to help meet these

Using a personal computer connected by modem to a minicomputer where the expert system is stored, the doctor has entered a description of a thirty-four-year-old male patient who has been suffering fevers, night sweats, and itching, and who has been losing weight; the doctor has also found an enlarged lymph node in the neck. The system returns a list of diseases that fit the bill, including two very rare possibilities: a fungal infection of the lungs called blastomycosis, and a viral infection picked up through a cat's scratch.

The system begins to refine the diagnosis by asking about a symptom linked to one of the possible diseases. Through the menu of responses, the doctor asks the system to explain its reasoning. The answer (bottom) helps him follow the course of the system's logic and may trigger ideas culled from personal experience or knowledge of the patient's medical history.

Having ruled out tonsillitis, the system follows a more ominous tack (below): Lymph nodes that are immobile may suggest cancer because cancerous lumps bind themselves to surrounding tissue as the cancer spreads.

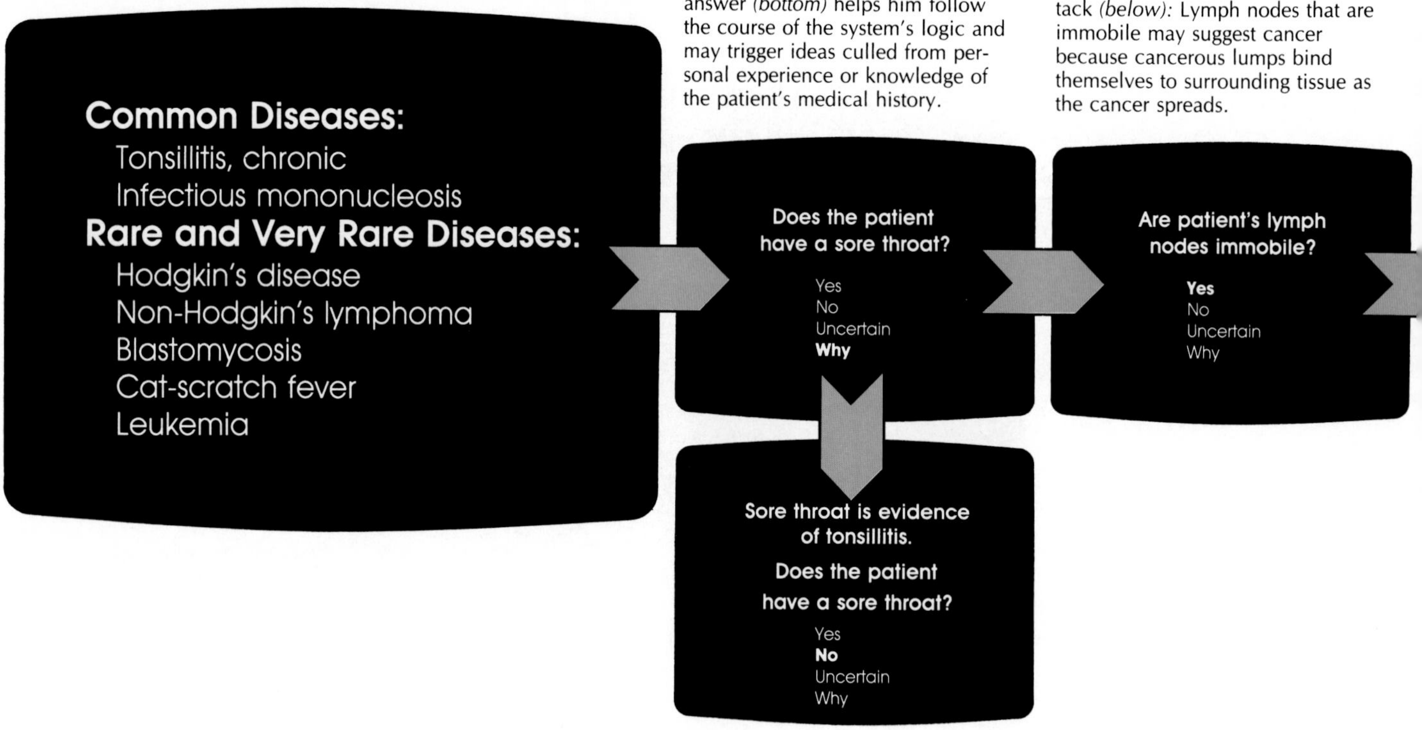

Common Diseases:
Tonsillitis, chronic
Infectious mononucleosis
Rare and Very Rare Diseases:
Hodgkin's disease
Non-Hodgkin's lymphoma
Blastomycosis
Cat-scratch fever
Leukemia

Does the patient have a sore throat?

Yes
No
Uncertain
Why

Are patient's lymph nodes immobile?

Yes
No
Uncertain
Why

Sore throat is evidence of tonsillitis.

Does the patient have a sore throat?

Yes
No
Uncertain
Why

demands. The system on which the simplified example below is based includes 2,000 diseases, 4,700 symptoms (called terms) and 65,000 disease-term relationships—the means by which the program's inference engine draws conclusions.

The process has two parts. Initially, by linking sets of symptoms with diseases and calculating probabilities, the program creates a ranked list of possible common and rare diseases. Then it begins interrogating the doctor, gathering more evidence that it can use to narrow and refine the search.

The goal is not absolute certainty but a fully explored list of possibilities. To that end, diagnostic expert systems are designed to allow the physician to pick the brains of the program, not just by demanding more information from the system's memory files but by asking questions that, for example, make the program justify its reasoning. As the refining process continues, the doctor gets a clear sense of what needs to be done, such as the ordering of further tests in order to achieve an even more definitive diagnosis.

The doctor's response to a further question about lymph nodes indicates that more evidence needs to be collected. Hilar lymph nodes, located in the center of the chest, can only be examined by x-ray, so the doctor knows to order one.

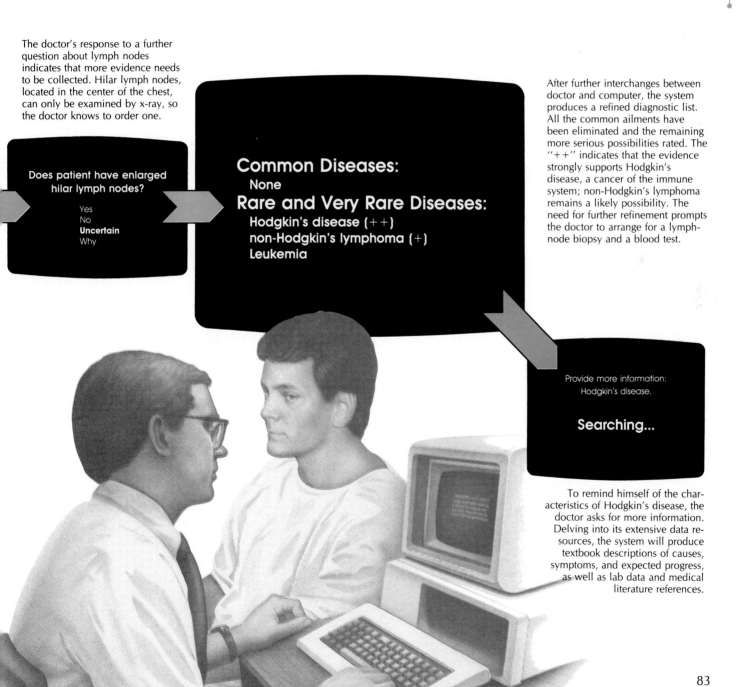

Does patient have enlarged hilar lymph nodes?

Yes
No
Uncertain
Why

Common Diseases:
None
Rare and Very Rare Diseases:
Hodgkin's disease (++)
non-Hodgkin's lymphoma (+)
Leukemia

After further interchanges between doctor and computer, the system produces a refined diagnostic list. All the common ailments have been eliminated and the remaining more serious possibilities rated. The "++" indicates that the evidence strongly supports Hodgkin's disease, a cancer of the immune system; non-Hodgkin's lymphoma remains a likely possibility. The need for further refinement prompts the doctor to arrange for a lymph-node biopsy and a blood test.

Provide more information:
Hodgkin's disease.

Searching...

To remind himself of the characteristics of Hodgkin's disease, the doctor asks for more information. Delving into its extensive data resources, the system will produce textbook descriptions of causes, symptoms, and expected progress, as well as lab data and medical literature references.

Pinning Down the Disease

The patient's case has passed, for the moment, into the hands of a pathologist, who will examine the biopsy sample—a thin slice of tissue from the abnormal lymph node—under a microscope. With the aid of a more specialized diagnostic expert system than the one explained on the previous pages, the pathologist will look for physical signs at the cellular level that point unmistakably to the presence of a specific disease.

Like more general expert systems, those used by pathologists walk the physician through a series of questions geared

In response to the answer "Few," the system displays on a color monitor a representative example of few RS cells, which appear in the image below as cells with double nuclei. On the text monitor *(bottom),* the system also indicates newly calculated probabilities.

Working from a list of significant tissue features identified by the expert system for the given type of biopsy sample and disease possibilities, the pathologist has chosen to focus on Reed-Sternberg (RS) cells and their variants. The system then prompts the pathologist to examine the sample and identify the number of RS cells present; their frequency is a key clue to the computer about the nature of the disease.

Having noted that the sample slide does not match the density of cells in his specimen, the pathologist gets the system to ask the question again so that he can change his answer *(below).* The system responds with a new diagnosis *(bottom):* The lymph node is definitely cancerous. The pathologist confirms by comparing his sample with a slide representing many RS cells *(bottom left).*

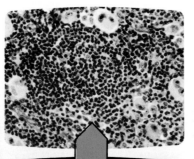

Feature Categories:
Follicles
Patterns
RS cells and variants
Large lymph cells
Small lymph cells

What is the number of RS cells?
Many
Few
Rare
Absent

Hodgkin's or
non-Hodgkin's lymphomas:
99% probability.

AIDS or
infectious mononucleosis:
1% probability.

What is the number
of RS cells?

Many
Few
Rare
Absent

Ruling out AIDS and mononucleosis:
focusing on lymphomas.

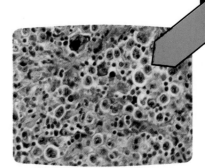

toward eliminating or confirming possibilities. However, they focus tightly on specific types of tissue; the example here, for examining lymphatic tissue, employs one of forty different knowledge bases within a single system. This specialization allows for a greater concentration of computing resources and a better chance of achieving a single correct diagnosis.

The pathologist's job is made difficult by the tremendous number and variety of cell features that must be identified and the similarity in appearance between benign and malignant manifestations. The lymph-node-pathology expert system helps by keeping track of more than 500 tissue features and linking them to dozens of diseases. But its most significant contribution is visual; a rich library of between five and ten thousand slides stored on videodisk allows the pathologist to compare the tissue sample at hand with images of representative samples and to identify differences. With the click of a mouse the pathologist can review on a TV monitor as many as thirty slides per feature at a range of magnification levels.

To distinguish between the two remaining disease alternatives, the expert system asks the pathologist to look for RS variants with only one nucleus. Though not shown here, more slides from the expert system's files would help the pathologist confirm by visual comparison that there are many mononuclear variants present.

The pathologist's response has led to a single possibility: The patient has Hodgkin's disease. But since there are eight types of Hodgkin's, the computer and the pathologist will continue to interact to reach a final conclusion, perhaps returning to the original list of tissue features *(far left)* in order to pursue evidence along other pathways.

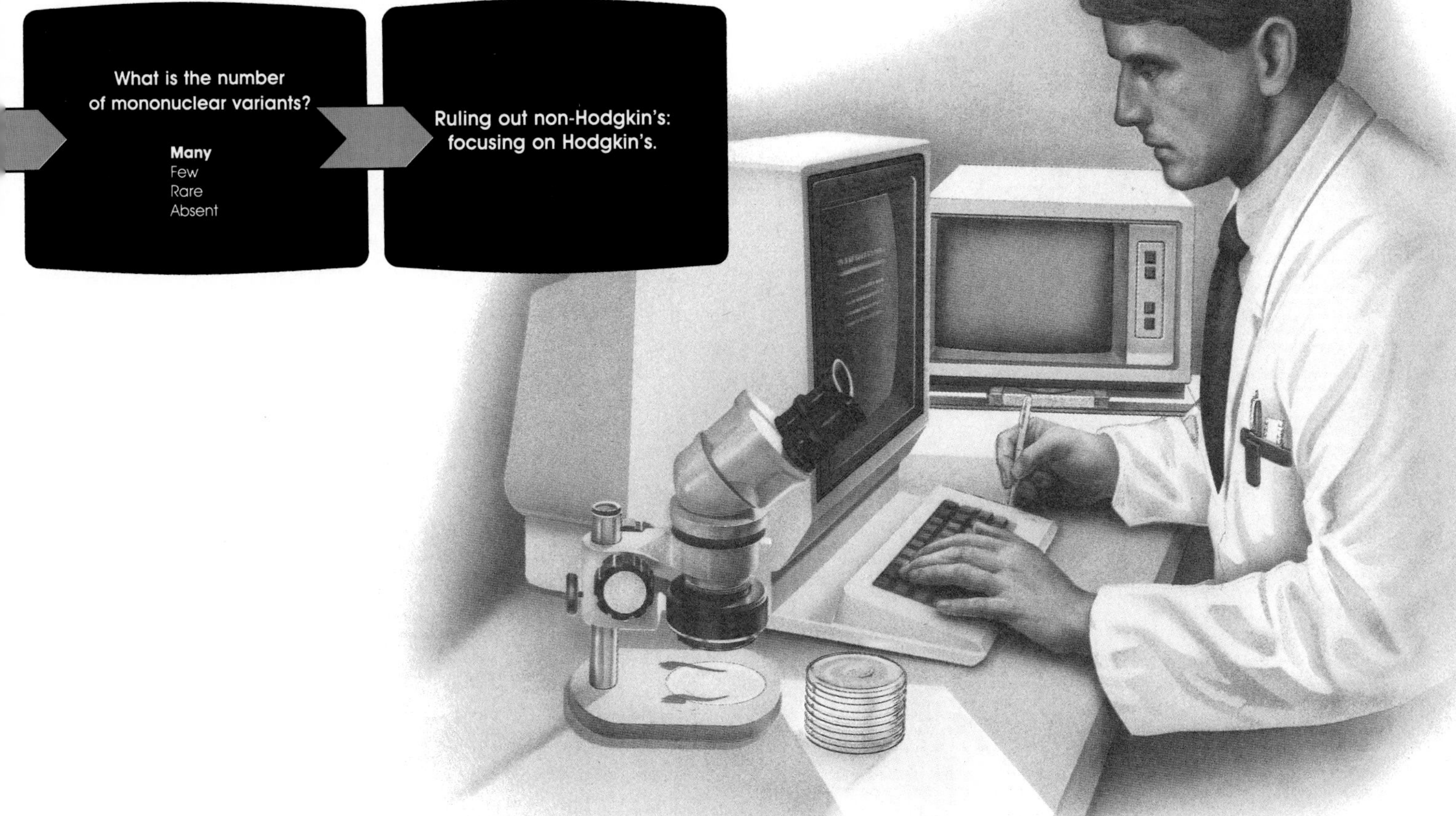

What is the number of mononuclear variants?

Many
Few
Rare
Absent

Ruling out non-Hodgkin's: focusing on Hodgkin's.

Expert Tracking of a Treatment Course

The conclusion of all the previous detective work is that the patient has Stage 2 Hodgkin's disease, indicating among other things that the cancer has spread to a second lymph node. To attack such a serious condition, a cancer specialist has chosen an intricate program of chemotherapy, using potent drugs to try to destroy cancerous cells. The sophistication and complexity of this experimental treatment, known as a chemotherapy protocol, confronts the physician with a mountain of

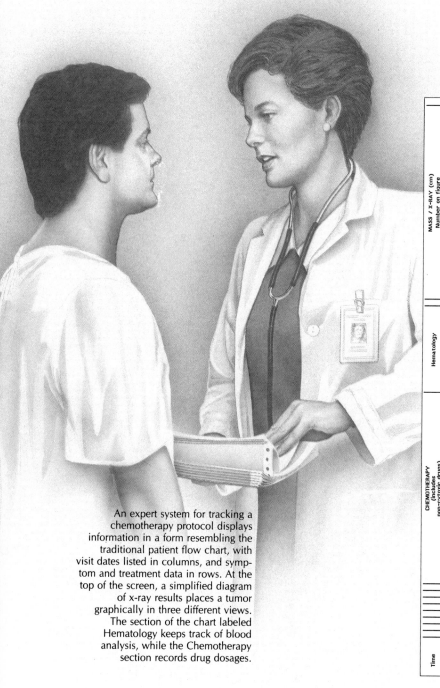

An expert system for tracking a chemotherapy protocol displays information in a form resembling the traditional patient flow chart, with visit dates listed in columns, and symptom and treatment data in rows. At the top of the screen, a simplified diagram of x-ray results places a tumor graphically in three different views. The section of the chart labeled Hematology keeps track of blood analysis, while the Chemotherapy section records drug dosages.

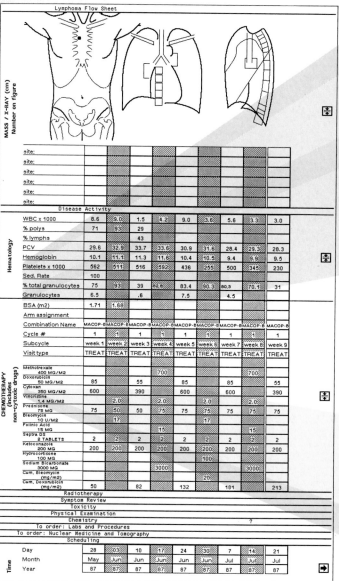

Lymphoma Flow Sheet

MASS / X-RAY (cm) Number on figure

site:									
site:									
site:									
site:									
site:									
site:									

Disease Activity

Hematology

WBC x 1000	8.6	9.0	1.5	4.2	9.0	3.6	5.6	3.3	3.0
% polys	71	93	29						
% lymphs			43						
PCV	29.6	32.9	33.7	33.6	30.9	31.6	28.4	29.3	28.3
Hemoglobin	10.1	11.1	11.3	11.6	10.4	10.5	9.4	9.9	9.5
Platelets x 1000	562	511	516	592	436	255	500	345	230
Sed. Rate	100								
% total granulocytes	75	93	39	82.8	83.4	90.3	80.3	70.1	31
Granulocytes	6.5		.6		7.5		4.5		

CHEMOTHERAPY (includes non-cytoxic drugs)

BSA (m2)	1.71	1.68							
Arm assignment									
Combination Name	MACOP-B	MACOP-B	MACOP-B	MACOP-B	MACOP-B	MACOP-B	MACOP-B	MACOP-B	MACOP-B
Cycle #	1	1	1	1	1	1	1	1	1
Subcycle	week 1	week 2	week 3	week 4	week 5	week 6	week 7	week 8	week 9
Visit type	TREAT	TREAT	TREAT	TREAT	TREAT	TREAT	TREAT	TREAT	TREAT
Methotrexate 400 MG/M2				700				700	
Doxorubicin 50 MG/M2	85		55		85		85		55
Cytoxan 350 MG/M2	600		390		600		600		390
Vincristine 1.4 MG/M2		2.0		2.0		2.0		2.0	
Prednisone 75 MG	75	50	50	75	75	75	75	75	75
Bleomycin 10 U/M2		17				17			
Folinic Acid 15 MG				15				15	
Septra DS 2 TABLETS	2	2	2	2	2	2	2	2	2
Ketoconazole 200 MG	200	200	200	200	200	200	200	200	200
Hydrocortisone 100 MG						100			
Sodium Bicarbonate 3000 MG				3000				3000	
Cum. Bleomycin (mg/m2)						20			
Cum. Doxorubicin (mg/m2)	50		82		132		181		213

Radiotherapy									
Symptom Review									
Toxicity									
Physical Examination									
Chemistry						?			
To order: Labs and Procedures									
To order: Nuclear Medicine and Tomography									
Scheduling									

Time

Day	28	03	10	17	24	30	7	14	21
Month	May	Jun	Jun	Jun	Jun	Jun	Jul	Jul	Jul
Year	87	87	87	87	87	87	87	87	87

minute but important details. Once again, an expert system represents an effective means of managing the information.

Accurate tracking of drugs administered and effects produced is crucial in chemotherapy because the highly toxic drugs involved attack healthy cells as well as cancerous ones. In addition, since protocols are experimental attempts to improve treatment, detailed records that are immediately accessible through computers can become a valuable re-source for researchers seeking to develop new techniques.

The simplified version of a cancer-treatment expert system illustrated below manages and organizes a variety of data entered by the physician, as well as advising on dosage adjustments based on the patient's response. Graphic displays and charts provide instantaneous reviews and help the physician keep on top of the situation throughout what will undoubtedly be a long course of treatment.

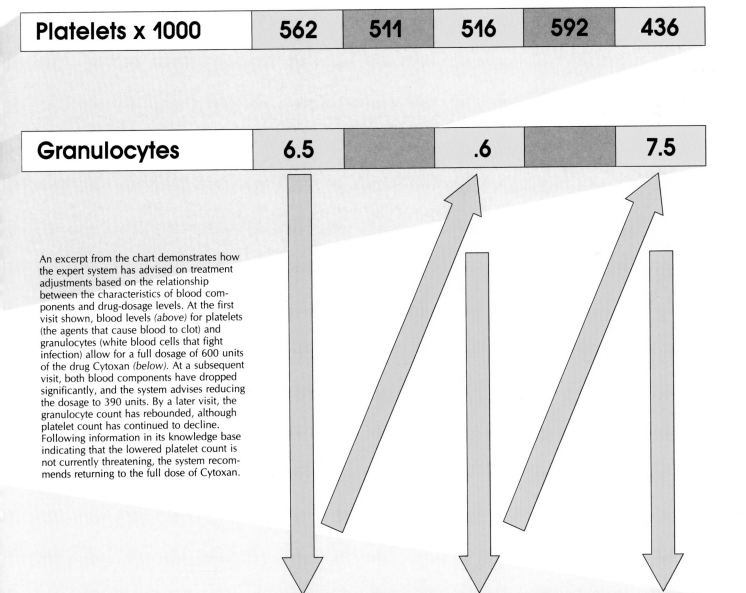

| Platelets x 1000 | 562 | 511 | 516 | 592 | 436 |

| Granulocytes | 6.5 | | .6 | | 7.5 |

An excerpt from the chart demonstrates how the expert system has advised on treatment adjustments based on the relationship between the characteristics of blood components and drug-dosage levels. At the first visit shown, blood levels (above) for platelets (the agents that cause blood to clot) and granulocytes (white blood cells that fight infection) allow for a full dosage of 600 units of the drug Cytoxan (below). At a subsequent visit, both blood components have dropped significantly, and the system advises reducing the dosage to 390 units. By a later visit, the granulocyte count has rebounded, although platelet count has continued to decline. Following information in its knowledge base indicating that the lowered platelet count is not currently threatening, the system recommends returning to the full dose of Cytoxan.

| Cytoxan 350 MG/M2 | 600 | | 390 | | 600 |

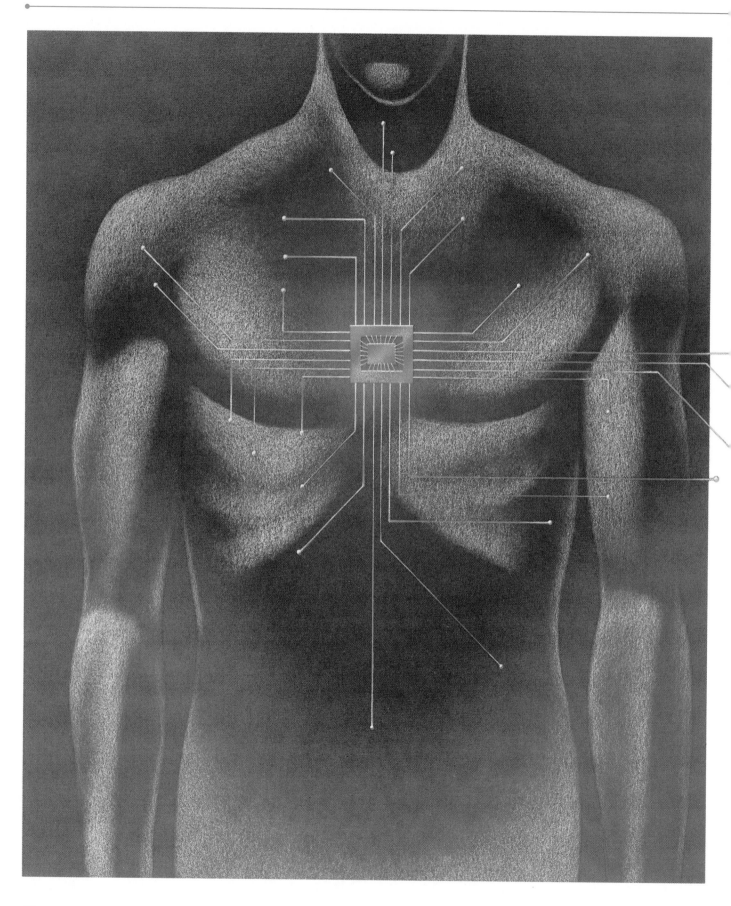

Electronic Surrogates

3

Stephen Hawking ranks among the greatest theoretical physicists of the century. Intellectually, he is relentlessly active; physically, he is almost helpless. On his own, he cannot walk, talk, or write. But aided by computers, he continues to work at the pinnacle of academe as Lucasian Professor of Mathematics at Cambridge University (the post once held by Isaac Newton and later by Charles Babbage, father of the computer). Hawking teaches, publishes articles and books, travels, and lectures, all at an impressive pace. During a two-month visit to California, for example, he delivered no fewer than fourteen lectures.

Hawking is merely the most famous person to benefit from a remarkable variety of computerized devices that now can make up for failings of the human body. Thousands of ordinary folk, handicapped by disease or genetics, rely on them. Computers keep time for erratic hearts, read books to the blind, deliver meaningful sound to the profoundly deaf, regulate the flow of life-giving insulin for diabetics, and communicate for people who are paralyzed and voiceless. Many of these aids are invisible. Fingernail-size microprocessors permit construction of devices so small they can be implanted within the body, where they remain undisturbed for years. Doctors adjust them by remote control—often relying on information the devices themselves have gathered for that purpose.

Impressive as these achievements are, they will almost certainly be eclipsed by electronic aids that are just beginning to take shape. Researchers have managed to create some vision directly through the optic nerve behind a blinded eye. Other experimenters have programmed computers to imitate the sequence of neural instructions that enable the body to move. The astonishing result: Paraplegic patients walk and even climb stairs under their own power through stimulation of their muscles with electric currents controlled by microprocessors.

Of the many computerized accessories now in regular use to assist the body, the most complex are those that permit people like Hawking to communicate with their fellows. Without computers, Hawking's prodigious mental powers would be locked in his head, lost forever. In another time he would have gradually disappeared from the academic and intellectual world as his physical abilities ebbed. Instead, an ingenious collection of computer components and software helps him carry on.

When Hawking was only twenty-one years old, his body began to deteriorate from amyotrophic lateral sclerosis (ALS, also known as Lou Gehrig's disease, after the 1930s baseball star who succumbed to it). ALS is an insidious, progressive nerve disorder. It gradually deprives its victims of control over muscles, first in the hands, then in the legs, and finally, even of vocal muscles.

Hawking developed the first symptoms of ALS shortly after he began his graduate work at Cambridge. He continued his studies from the confines of a wheelchair, received a doctorate in physics, and took a teaching post at Cambridge. A once-indifferent student, he set out in headlong pursuit of the most elusive quarry of theoretical physicists—a grand unified theory that would combine all known laws of the workings of the universe into one logical package. It was as if he was working to beat the clock, one colleague recalls.

Over the next few years, Hawking's upper body gradually weakened. His everyday needs—eating, bathing, dressing—were met by nurses and family. He required help even to thumb through books and research papers. He could control movement in only three fingers. As vocal muscles failed, his speech became slurred, understandable only by his family, students, and closest colleagues. Then, during a trip to Switzerland in 1985, he contracted pneumonia, and doctors were forced to implant a permanent breathing tube in his throat. The life-saving tube cost Hawking all remaining speech. Lacking a voice and without strength to write, his mind was caged.

His rescuer was David Mason, a Cambridge engineer and the husband of one of Hawking's nurses. Using off-the-shelf components, Mason put together a system that made Hawking once again communicative. Its core is a Datavue 25 computer and speech synthesizer housed in a box on the back of Hawking's motorized wheelchair and powered by batteries under the chair's seat. A flat, compact liquid-crystal display screen is mounted on the left arm of the chair. To operate the system, Hawking squeezes a switch six inches long and a half-inch thick with two fingers of his right hand. The software—appropriately known as The Equalizer—was developed at Words +, Inc., in Lancaster, California, by Walt Woltosz, whose mother suffered from ALS. It has one drawback, says Englishman Hawking of its speech synthesis: "I hope you will agree my voice is clear and easy to understand. The only trouble is my American accent."

The Equalizer software operates in a way familiar to any computer user. When Hawking starts up the system, the screen is split into three parts. The upper half is devoted to the main menu; the bottom half is divided into two work areas, one

The eminent British astrophysicist Stephen Hawking, disabled by the neurological disorder known as Lou Gehrig's disease, navigates the world in his computer-equipped wheelchair. A joystick controls the chair's movements. With his right hand, Hawking operates a switch that allows him to build sentences from a menu of words displayed on the screen in front of him; the computer then speaks on his behalf with a voice generator.

for speaking, the other for writing. The fourteen-line, six-column menu offers the letters of the alphabet, with which he can spell out words or select from a stored vocabulary. The display also includes the five most frequently used word endings in the English language *(er, ly, ing, s,* and *d/ed),* and a series of command options for writing, editing, and speaking. In addition, the top line contains words that are complete thoughts in themselves and can be spoken instantly: "yes," "no," "maybe," "I don't know," and "thanks." And the menu's last six lines supply so-called QuikWords, the thirty-six most frequently used words in the English language—such as "I," "to," "they," and "my"—that make up about 40 percent of normal conversation.

Using the system is something like centering the cross hairs of a gun sight on the desired word or command. First, the program scans down the lines of the menu, highlighting them one at a time. When it reaches the line Hawking wants, he squeezes the switch to freeze the scan and begin another, moving in the selected line across the columns of commands and words. When the desired point is highlighted, Hawking stops the scan with another squeeze. If he has chosen a command, it is executed; if he has indicated a word, it is moved automatically into one of the work areas. Words are assembled there into the text and held until Hawking sends it on to be stored.

Hawking does not have to spell out each word he writes; the program contains a 2,750-word vocabulary stored alphabetically, large enough even for one with Hawking's intellectual range. When he selects a letter from the menu's alphabet—*A* for instance—the program immediately begins displaying the *A* portion of its vocabulary, one screen at a time. When Hawking stops at a screen, the horizontal and vertical scans begin so that he can select the word he needs. When necessary, he can flip back to the alphabet to build a word letter by letter.

Another feature of the software is word prediction. The system learns Hawking's word pattern—which words he uses most often in connection with other words—and retains them in memory. As he writes, the computer displays and highlights the six words he is most likely to want next. With such computerized prompting, Hawking can write at a rate of fifteen to twenty words a minute.

But Hawking must also work and teach in the special language of mathematics, and so he must write complex equations that use Greek characters and special symbols. For this purpose, Hawking has a program called TEX, which allows him to create equations in words. These are then translated into the traditional form of mathematics.

Hawking can store his composition on a disk, print it, or "speak" it out loud with his voice synthesizer. He prepares lectures weeks ahead of time and stores them until his presentation. He can conduct a running conversation by selecting words a few at a time and sending them off to the synthesizer, which voices them immediately.

The system that enables Stephen Hawking to communicate was adapted to his unique needs, but simpler versions are used by hundreds of other people similarly handicapped. Engineer David Mason, for example, has made near-duplicates of the Hawking unit (cost: about $8,000 each), and several versions of the Words + software are widely sold ($2,000 and up). All serve the same purpose, but they may include interesting variations to suit the user's physical disability. The control mechanism, for example, is crucial. Hawking's controller, operated by a gentle squeeze, is conventional in operation and concept. Many others exploit diverse capacities of the human body. There are "puff 'n' sip" switches, controlled by blowing or sipping on a tube. Some switches are operated by pressure from the chin, nose, toes, or even eyebrows. Oversized keyboards are used by those whose hands shake uncontrollably and undersize ones by those with limited movement. And one of the most ingeniously contrived switches can be operated by a mere glance, restoring a measure of control to the most severely constrained body.

ERICA'S EYE
Even totally paralyzed people generally can move their eyes. This fact has been put to use in ERICA (Eyegaze Response Interface Computer Aid), a device that requires a computer of its own to direct its operations.

ERICA is the brainchild of Thomas Hutchinson, an energetic professor of biomedical engineering at the University of Virginia in Charlottesville. In 1984, Hutchinson visited Children's (now Kluge) Medical Center in Charlottesville, where he was appalled by the plight of quadriplegic youngsters. Many of them could not speak or move; they were cut off from the world, unable to communicate or even call for help. The visit had a special impact on Hutchinson: A high-school football injury had rendered him similarly helpless for three days, long enough to understand the pain and frustration of the afflicted children.

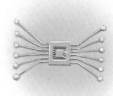

Without exception, these young patients were able to control the movement of their eyes. Hutchinson had seen how much computers helped other disabled persons, and he felt they could help these children too, if the youngsters' eyes could somehow be used to control a computer. A reflection of light in an animal's eyes gave him a clue to the way this might be accomplished. He reasoned that if a computer could be trained to recognize and measure a similar reflection from a child's eyes, perhaps it could tell where that child was looking.

He chose to work with infrared light because it would be unnoticeable and would not damage the eye. For an infrared source, he found a $1.49 light-emitting diode in a neighborhood electronics store. He mounted the light in the middle of the lens of a small video camera, which he modified to be sensitive only to infrared light, and connected the camera to a video processor board mounted in a standard personal computer. The eye's reflection of the infrared beam would be picked up by the video camera and converted to digital signals by the video processor; a computer program written by Hutchinson would teach the computer to recognize the reflection.

DOUBLE IMAGES
At this stage, the system could only tell if the light was being reflected back into the camera. It could not tell whether the reflection came from an eye or a mirror. And if it did come from an eye, there was no way to tell where the eye was looking. For this information, Hutchinson needed two reflections, and he found them: one from the surface of the eyeball and the other from the retina, at the back of the eye. The marked difference in curvature between the eye's two

surfaces, and the slight but measurable difference in their distances from the light cause the two reflections to fall upon the camera's lens at slightly different angles. The ERICA computer measures those angles, and from them it calculates where the user is looking. The system is sensitive enough to detect eye movements of as little as an inch across a computer screen. The screen is divided into thirty-six separate areas about one-and-one-half-inches square, each one representing a choice of a word or action. In effect, the paired reflections act like a mouse, telling the computer what to do.

In use, ERICA's camera and infrared light look out from beneath the computer screen. They scan in a spiral pattern in front of the screen, seeking a reflection. When one is received, the computer searches the digitized image for a second reflection—the clue that an eye is watching. If only one reflection is there, the camera resumes its search. When the computer detects the glint of an eye, it instructs the camera to track the paired reflections and leads the user through a series of steps that fit the system to the person, compensating for differences in the reflection angles caused by body size and position. To accomplish this compensation, the computer measures the angle between the two reflections as the user looks at each corner of the screen. With those positions fixed, the computer is able to interpolate the angles that will indicate when this user is looking at points in between. In this way, ERICA can be fitted to a person who is short or tall, and who is standing, sitting, or reclining; no other special adjustments or equipment are needed.

A half-second gaze is sufficient to choose a word or execute a command. At the end of a quarter-second, the computer sounds an alert that it is about to interpret the gaze as an intended order, and if the gaze continues for another quarter-second, the word is chosen or acted on.

ERICA can be connected to almost any device that is switch-operated. Hutchinson's paraplegic patients are able to select foods and beverages from a menu, turn on lights and appliances, play video games, write messages with a word processor, and even control a music synthesizer. Because Hutchinson remembers his own days of paralyzed pain, he also included a program that enables an ERICA user to sound an alarm for immediate help.

A READING MACHINE

By enabling paralyzed people to convey information, ERICA and other switch-operated word processors and speech synthesizers address one side of the communications problem: the output side. But there is another side: input. The blind and the deaf have difficulty acquiring information, not disseminating it. And for them—far greater in number than the paralyzed—computerized aids again have worked wonders.

For those without the gift of sight, inability to read is a severe handicap. The Braille language helps. Since its introduction in the early nineteenth century, it has been an indispensable tool of the blind, enabling them to read by feeling the patterns of raised dots on a page. It has since been supplemented by recordings of printed matter. But Braille and recorded matter amount to only a small fraction of the knowledge resources available to sighted people.

A large step toward remedying that situation was taken in 1975, when a device called a reading machine brought together two relatively new technologies—

pattern recognition and voice synthesis—in a single unit that could read any book or magazine article to the blind. The reading machine was not only a significant development in computing, it was also a conceptual break from the past. Until that time, most uses of computers by the blind dealt with ways to produce output in Braille or to have a voice synthesizer speak the contents of a computer screen. But the reading machine's creator, an M.I.T. graduate student named Raymond Kurzweil, saw the possibility of a broader and more direct print-to-mind path.

An accomplished computer programmer since his early teens, Kurzweil was intrigued with artificial intelligence (AI). He recalls, "Getting a machine to recognize letters and words on a page is a classic problem in AI research, and I had a technique I thought would work. A reading machine for the blind seemed the most promising application to begin with." True enough—but a daunting challenge. At the time, computer scientists had not made much headway in the field of optical scanning and character recognition. The

Pop musician Stevie Wonder gives an impromptu performance for Raymond Kurzweil, designer of his synthesizer. The computerized sound-generating device can mimic any musical instrument—and also simulate many instruments playing at once. This particular instrument is equipped with a speech synthesizer that tells the composer, who is blind, how he has set the keyboard's controls.

available devices could read only a single style of print, and then slowly. Often, the only way to make materials machine-readable was to transcribe them manually into one of the few typefaces legible with a particular machine. The need for transcription, of course, was what limited the supply of Braille and recorded materials to the blind—the very restraint Kurzweil wanted to overcome.

It took him two years to do it, but the Kurzweil Reading Machine, first installed at the Perkins School for the Blind in Watertown, Massachusetts, in 1976, worked wonderfully. It looked much like a copying machine: a large box topped by a glass plate on which books or documents were placed face down. At the press of a button a scanner moved across the page and, within seconds, a voice began reciting the contents. Some called it the first significant new aid for the blind since 1829, when Braille was invented.

Kurzweil himself was not so easily impressed. The instrument weighed 350 pounds and cost $50,000, much too large and expensive to be widely useful. Within a decade, however, Kurzweil trimmed the weight to 20 pounds, reduced the price to $8,000, and added a host of features—including a portable version. The Personal Reader, as the portable machine is called, reads virtually any printed or typewritten page in ninety seconds, speaks at up to 350 words per minute, and has such extras as a talking calculator and an electronic "bookmark" that permits the user to jump back and forth within a text. It can also be connected to another computer, to become a talking word processor. To forestall the possibility of boredom when listening to long readings, the machine's users can switch at will between nine synthesized voices—four men, four women, and one friendly child, dubbed Kit the Kid.

A HOST OF EXPERTS

The heart of the Personal Reader is Kurzweil's character-recognition software, which he describes as a group of "experts," each with a separate specialty, whose actions are coordinated by an electronic manager. Each of the resident experts works on a single recognition task. For example, one detects loops (the form found in the letters A and B). Another looks for concavities, such as that at the bottom of the letter A. These two experts enable the program to conclude, for instance, that a symbol with one loop and a concavity is probably an A.

Distinguishing the letter H from N is a bit more difficult. Both consist of three straight lines and concavities at the top and bottom. So other experts recognize and count straight lines and measure the position and angles of lines, loops, and concavities. Some make it possible for the program to see that an H has a horizontal bar in the center, while an N contains a diagonal bar; others recognize that, while the number 8 is symmetrical, the letter B is not. Still other experts specialize in the rules of spelling and grammar; some examine the context of each character—distinguishing the letter O from a zero, for example—and help decipher typographical errors and broken type.

As wondrous as all this activity is, close examination of every character by a panel of electronic wizards takes time. In order to speed things up, Kurzweil devised a way to make the Reading Machine learn as it scans, so its performance improves with every page of a document.

Learning is accomplished with yet another group of experts, low-level ones that can be taught to recognize whole characters rapidly after the more complex high-level experts have completed examination of the loops, concavities, and other features of the typeface found in a particular document. Once the machine understands that an *A* and a *B* have certain shapes in the document it is examining, the low-level experts can be called back in to analyze the text. Thus accuracy is not sacrificed. Altogether, the system uses more than a thousand rules of language—and 1,500 exceptions to those rules—to group the characters into words that can be passed along and read out loud by the speech synthesizer.

THE ELECTRONIC EAR

Less complex than computers that read for the blind—but no less valuable—are those that hear for the deaf. Sight is priceless, but hearing is in some ways a more essential avenue of communication. To make up for loss of this crucial sense, the electronic hearing aid has been available for more than half a century. But until the advent of microprocessors, hearing aids were sometimes considered as much a bother as a boon by their users. The reason is simple: The hearing aid was unable to do what the ear and brain together can do—distinguish the sounds a person wants to hear from the rest of the world's noise.

A hearing aid in its most basic form does its job simply by amplifying sound enough to overcome its wearer's disability: It furnishes an electronic shout. In this form, however, the aid amplifies all the sounds that reach it. If the only one is that of a voice in a quiet room, the hearing aid's user will hear the voice clearly. But when the speaker's voice is one of many sounds in a crowded room, the user will have difficulty distinguishing it from the background clutter.

The nature of deafness contributes to the clutter problem: Most people lose hearing in only part of the spectrum; their hearing remains largely intact at some frequen-

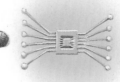

cies. When a conventional hearing aid amplifies, it boosts nearly all frequencies equally, sometimes burying the desired sound in a blast of unwanted noise. As a consequence, wearers of conventional devices find it necessary to adjust the volume of their hearing aids constantly.

Dramatically better performance is provided by a tiny computerized aid—the zeta noise blocker—that cuts through the babble of a crowded room and delivers understandable speech to its user. The device, developed in 1987 by Daniel Graupe of the University of Illinois at Chicago, separates background noise from speech by analyzing sound patterns. Speech is characterized by a rising and falling of volume and pitch, while noise tends to be a steady blur of sound. The computer seeks out the different patterns and activates filters that suppress noise frequencies and reinforce conversational tones.

The patterns are distinguished by mathematical analysis that separates a sound wave into its many component waves. (Even the sound of a piano note is not a single frequency but the sum of several.) To accomplish this breakdown, the computerized hearing aid must first convert the composite sound wave from its continuously varying analog form into the discrete pulses of a digital signal. Only then can the component frequencies be identified, the undesirable ones recognized and discarded, and the remaining ones reconstructed into a new component wave—an understandable, useful sound. All this must be done so quickly that there is no perceptible time lag.

The mathematical techniques to accomplish this separation and reconstruction are very complex. One method, called Fourier analysis, can require hundreds of thousands of calculations to break a simple sound wave into a few components. Even the most up-to-date microchips are hard-pressed to fill this order quickly enough: The microprocessors in the zeta noise blocker and similar computerized hearing aids are among the hardest-working electronic devices in common use.

While noise blocking alone vastly improves hearing-aid performance, other improvements have also been made. Designers have contrived ways to reduce the amount of work the computer must do by carefully matching the hearing aid to the wearer's needs, then dividing those needs into separate programs that the wearer can select to suit particular conditions. This enables the computer to concentrate on doing one task extremely well, rather than diffusing its talents. For example, a program tailored for telephone conversation devotes the full capacity of the computer to manipulating the narrow range of sound frequencies that the phone transmits, without wasting valuable computing power trying to find and analyze other sounds.

One such hearing aid, the MemoryMate, developed by the 3M Corporation, has a capacity of eight programs. Each program can be tailored to enhance the wearer's hearing in a particular situation—listening to music, telephone conversation, or speech in a noisy room, for example. The aid is customized for its user in the doctor's office. The doctor positions a tiny microphone near the eardrum, fits the MemoryMate in place, then runs tests that are analyzed by a special computer; from the microphone, the doctor's computer hears the sound produced by the MemoryMate just as it is heard by the user. This feedback allows a signal analyzer to calculate how well the aid is meeting the patient's actual needs. The aid can be reprogrammed and retested until its output is satisfactory.

IMPLANTED AIDS

These advances in technology work only for those who retain some natural hearing. Unfortunately, some cases of deafness cannot be helped by the most sophisticated aids because disease or birth defects have severely damaged the delicate interaction of mechanical, chemical, and electrical forces that produce hearing. Yet even such profoundly deaf people have now recovered some hearing with so-called cochlear implants, which administer bursts of electricity, rather than sound, to stimulate auditory nerves. These implants are not so much aids as replacements for parts of the ear, feeding the electrical equivalent of sound directly to the nerves that go to the hearing center of the brain.

In a healthy ear, those nerves are at the end of a complicated chain reaction. It begins when sound—actually, a pulse of air pressure—travels down the ear canal to the eardrum, the thin membrane that protects the middle and inner ear. The drum responds by vibrating against three tiny bones called the ossicles, which amplify the vibrations and transmit them to the fluid-filled spiral nerve center of the ear, the cochlea. There, the vibrations are further amplified and passed on to a system of still more membranes and 25,000 hairs, whose motion signals the intensity and frequency of the sound to the auditory nerve. Any disruption in that chain can cause deafness.

As early as the 1950s, before computers were widely used for medical research, scientists were trying to bypass the eardrum and ossicles and stimulate nerve endings deep within the cochlea. In 1978, a team of British surgeons working at the University of Melbourne in Australia implanted ten platinum electrodes in the cochlea of a man who had been totally deaf. The electrodes transmitted minute electric pulses generated by a computer-guided device on the man's belt—and restored his ability to distinguish many sounds.

Within a decade, more than 2,000 persons had been fitted with similar devices. A few users are enabled to hear well enough to carry on normal conversation. The majority, however, receive just an awareness of sound—a "neural event" that is somehow different from normal hearing but is a signal that sound is present. Medical research has shed little light on why some recipients of cochlear implants can hear and others cannot. Although information exists about the kind of electrical pulses that will stimulate the cochlear nerve endings, several key questions remain unanswered: Are some nerve endings more important than others? If so, which ones? How much stimulation is needed to produce intelligible hearing?

A man paralyzed below the neck accepts a drink from a robotic arm that responds to the spoken word. A voice-recognition system translates his commands into a digital language understood by the eight computers that govern the robot's movements. The device, known as the Robotic Aid, has been under development since 1981 by engineers at California's Stanford University and Veterans Administration Medical Center.

In operation, the cochlear implant shuttles sound and signals among three devices—one inside and two worn outside the body—before electrical pulses reach the implanted electrodes. The stimulator that generates the signals is buried with the electrodes within the ear. However, much of the processing takes place outside. A microphone behind the ear picks up sound and sends it by wire to the microprocessor, a box about the size of a deck of cards worn in a pocket or on the belt. Here the sounds are analyzed and instructions for the device's electronic stimulator are dispatched back to the earpiece, where a tiny radio transmitter signals the stimulator to send pulses on to the nerve endings.

Even though the device is cumbersome and the sensation it produces is far from natural sound, there is promise in the future: Computer scientists say it is within their ability to produce an implant that would create clear hearing—if only they understood more about the ear's workings.

MAINTAINING THE PACE

Gaps in knowledge of human physiology have not been the problem that delayed aids for two other kinds of human ills—failures of the heart and the pancreas. Although the workings of the heart, for example, have been well understood for many years, pacemakers to regulate its pumping action were only introduced in the 1950s, when the transistor made reliable miniature electronic circuits possible. It took another three decades for computer technology to catch up with medical knowledge. Today, this device, which started as a simple metronome for ailing hearts, has become more like an orchestra conductor, synchronizing the work of the heart's several chambers and adjusting the beat to suit the wearer's activity.

The pacemaker sets a steady rhythm for those whose hearts are unable to do so on their own, owing to injury, disease, or hereditary factors. Their irregular heartbeats limit physical activity, produce discomfort and can even threaten life. To restore normal rhythm, the pacemaker delivers small jolts of electricity to the heart muscle at precisely timed intervals, triggering the muscle to pump exactly when it should. The entire device, about two inches square, is surgically implanted in the chest wall and can be left to do its work until it is time to replace its batteries—about every five years.

Early pacemakers had many shortcomings arising out of the heart's complexity. This remarkable organ contains two major pumping chambers (the left and right ventricles), two priming chambers (the left and right auricles), and four valves that work in perfect synchronization in a healthy person. Blood from the body enters the right side of the heart, where it is pumped into the lungs. From the lungs, the blood returns to the powerful left side of the heart, which pumps it through the rest of the body. The synchronization of each auricle—the primer—with its ventricle is especially important; a priming pulse that is too soon or too late reduces the amount of blood the ventricle will pump.

The first pacemakers stimulated only the left ventricle, not the auricle. As a result, some pacemaker wearers continued to experience fatigue and discomfort despite the efforts of the machine. In the late 1970s, a microprocessor was used to synchronize pulses of both chambers of the heart. There soon followed more-sophisticated programs for these processors. One compensated for erratic heart action. First, it listened for a priming pulse from the auricle. If that was forthcoming, the computer sent a timed pulse to the ventricle; if no priming pulse was detected, the pacemaker supplied one. Other, ever-more-complex devices were developed, some supplying precise timing pulses for all four chambers.

INTERPRETING THE WORKLOAD

Despite these advances, many pacemaker wearers were still consigned to a sedentary life. Even the most complex cardiac metronome worked at a fixed pace. In early models, this rate was set before the device was implanted and could not be changed without surgery. By the 1960s, some models could be reset by sending a radio signal through the chest wall. But even this advance did not provide for the minute-to-minute variations in rate needed to compensate for physical activity. Just a walk around the block could leave a pacemaker user fatigued and short of breath. The cure, of course, lay in finding a sensing mechanism that could detect the need for a faster heart rate—and a processor that could produce it on demand.

This device was developed in the mid-1980s, when Neal Fearnot, a professor of biomedical engineering at Purdue University in Indiana, settled on blood temperature as the proper measure of bodily activity. He found that, among several indicators of muscle activity, such as changes in blood acidity and breathing rate, blood temperature was the most reliable and accurate. Blood not only supplies oxygen to the body's tissues, it also carries away heat created by their work. Thus, blood temperature rises and falls as bodily activity speeds and slows. Fearnot experimented with hundreds of animals

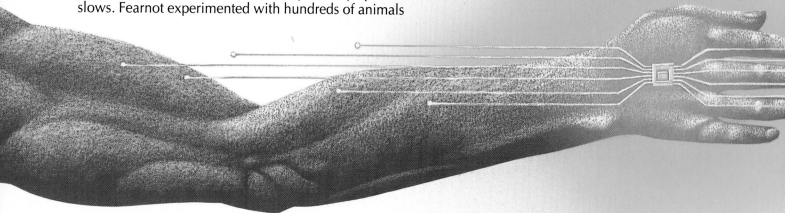

and human volunteers to develop a mathematical formula that describes the relationship between temperature and activity. With the formula in hand, he could program a pacemaker to react to a tiny sensor that constantly reads blood temperature. The sensor is located within the right auricle, which receives blood directly from the body.

Fearnot's variable-rate pacemaker is a two-inch-round package that contains battery, pulse generator, computer, and a tiny radio transmitter and receiver. The unit must be programmed by a cardiologist after implantation in order to match its functioning to the user's heart. The radio exchanges information and instructions about temperature and heart action with a computer on the doctor's desk.

The doctor's computer simulates the workings of the patient's heart, calculates the proper rhythm for various levels of activity, then transmits this prescription to the microprocessor, setting the program. Readjustments can be made later, if necessary, by repeating the process.

The pacemaker is first alerted to a step-up in activity when blood temperature drops abruptly—the first sign that the body is working harder. Soon the temperature rises, however, and the pacing rate rises with it, but no further than an upper limit set by the doctor—usually 110 to 120 beats per minute. When exertion ends and the blood begins cooling, the pacemaker gradually reduces the heartbeat to the resting level.

SWEET SUCCESS

In 1986, as Fearnot was putting the finishing touches on his pacemaker, doctors at Johns Hopkins University in Baltimore introduced a computerized device to compensate for failures of a different organ: the pancreas, which regulates the amount of sugar carried in the blood.

This sugar—glucose—is the body's fuel. In a healthy person, the pancreas maintains the proper level of glucose by producing the hormone called insulin. When the blood contains more sugar than the body needs, the insulin absorbs the excess. When the sugar level returns to normal, insulin production ceases. Insulin production is also restricted when a person is physically or emotionally stressed; this raises the sugar level, supplying the necessary extra energy.

In a diabetic, the pancreas produces too little insulin; hence the body is deprived of the ability to regulate blood sugar. Unless insulin is replaced artificially, the blood sugar level will rise, poison the diabetic, and without treatment, produce coma and death. Too high a dose of insulin to compensate for the inactive pancreas can have similar, equally devastating, results.

Because control over the balance of blood sugar and insulin must be precise, diabetics have to be constantly on the alert. Blood sugar must be monitored at least daily, and meals and exercise must be carefully planned. Insulin—normally taken by injections—must be coordinated with meals, which increase the sugar level, and exercise, which reduces it. Insulin control requires great discipline, and even then, stress and unplanned changes in schedule make occasional emergencies almost a certainty.

In effect, the Johns Hopkins device replaces the nonfunctioning pancreas. Called the Programmable Implantable Medication System (PIMS), it is a computer-controlled pump that enables diabetics to administer precise doses of insulin without the need for daily—or more frequent—injections. Instead, the insulin comes from a built-in reservoir that is refilled by injection about once a month. Because it does not monitor blood sugar the way a cardiac pacemaker reads temperature, the device is only partially automatic, requiring some control by the user.

The PIMS is programmed after it is implanted in the patient's abdomen. Blood tests are taken in the doctor's office, and a computer analyzes them and prescribes insulin doses to match the patient's needs. The device's internal processor is given a so-called basal rate at which it administers insulin in very small, regular doses sufficient for average, between-meal requirements. To correspond to mealtimes, when blood sugar rises sharply, as many as six additional doses can be released. (Diabetics are encouraged to eat many small meals, thus limiting the swing from high to low sugar levels.) The schedule can also be set to reduce the basal rate at times of especially low sugar levels and activity—during sleep, for example. The diabetic can override or modify the PIMS schedule with a pocket programmer to compensate for variations in normal activity. For example, the after-lunch dose could be delayed to adjust for a late meal.

ELECTRIFIED MOBILITY

While some physicians work on computerized replacements for human organs, others are seeking ways to furnish the spark of life directly to disabled bodies —quite literally so.

Scientists have long known that muscles are made to move by electricity. In 1744, Johannes Krüger at the University of Halle in Germany speculated that electricity might one day be used to "reestablish the power of motion" in paralyzed limbs. This idea was soon put into action. Although the would-be healers did not have any idea what electricity was, they experimented enthusiastically on patients paralyzed by strokes or spinal injuries, shocking muscles with charges produced by everything from primitive generators to electric eels. But since they lacked a means to control the stimuli, the experimenters produced only spasms—a far cry from the precisely choreographed movements that enable healthy people to grasp a book or walk across a room.

The difficulty of achieving electronic mobility lies in the great complexity of even the simplest bodily movement. Walking requires the coordinated action of scores of muscles, not only in the legs but also in the hips and upper body. It also depends on feedback. Information about the position of the body and the movement of every muscle is sent to the brain and continuously analyzed so that new instructions can be issued to keep the body erect and safely balanced.

Not until the early 1970s, when the computer was employed in attempts to aid the disabled, could researchers hope that they might control and synchronize electrical signals that would enable their patients to arise and walk away from wheelchairs and braces. In the decades since, the restoration of independent mobility has been achieved, but only experimentally. Electronic stimulation is demanding of both scientists and subjects. A crude imitation of natural walking requires a system of dozens of electrodes to stimulate muscles, and a network of sensors for feedback. Once this paraphernalia is implanted or attached, its use requires strength and intense concentration. An electrically assisted paraplegic cannot even stand without braces for more than five to ten minutes before muscles become exhausted. Walking requires even greater effort.

TIMING IS EVERYTHING

Nevertheless, each year a little more is accomplished. Computers become more powerful and more portable; doctors learn more about the working of muscles and the feedback needed to help them function.

One of the most successful recent efforts to realize Krüger's goal began in the early 1970s at Case Western Reserve University and the Veterans Administration Medical Center in Cleveland. There, a team headed by Dr. E. Byron Marsolais started out by implanting electrodes in a man's arm, sequencing the pulses with a mechanical timer. This crude rig worked well enough to convince

The Shapes of Things Within

Radiologists have long been accustomed to mentally piecing together a three-dimensional picture of a patient's internal organs, muscles, and bones from two-dimensional CT and MRI scans of the human body *(pages 45-57)*. An imaging technique called volume rendering now permits the assembling to be done by a computer instead of the physician.

Derived from special-effects software developed for the movie industry and made practical by speedy computers, volume rendering is a versatile tool, yielding results of unprecedented accuracy and clarity. It allows a doctor to color internal structures so that one can be distinguished from another, to render skin and muscle transparent so that deeper structures become visible, and to examine the resulting image from any viewpoint.

Volume rendering makes the outcome of surgery more predictable by allowing the surgeon to see the seat and extent of disease before operating. The technique preserves detail that would be lost with other imaging processes. A cancer specialist, for example, can see the position of a tumor in relation to other organs, making surgery or radiation therapy easier to plan.

An orthopedist with a patient complaining of a painful joint is able to determine whether the ailment is bursitis, arthritis, or a hairline fracture. The doctor can then judge whether surgery is appropriate, and if so, whether the operation will be a relatively minor one—arthroscopy on a twisted knee, for instance—or a major undertaking, such as the replacement of the patient's hip joint.

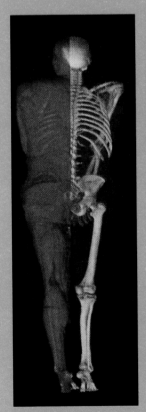 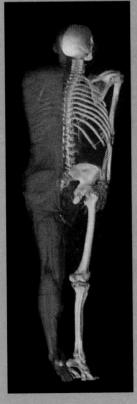 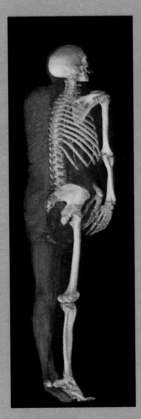 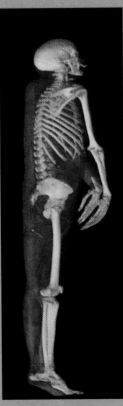 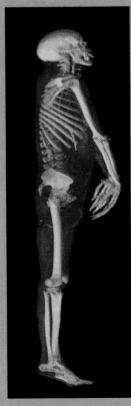

Multiple views of muscle and bone. The images above, created from 631 CT scans, show five views of a cadaver. The computer can reproduce muscle in fine detail or strip it away entirely to reveal skeletal structure. The computer has been instructed to make everything on one side of the figure transparent except bone. On the other side, muscle has been made opaque, with bone visible through the thinner layers.

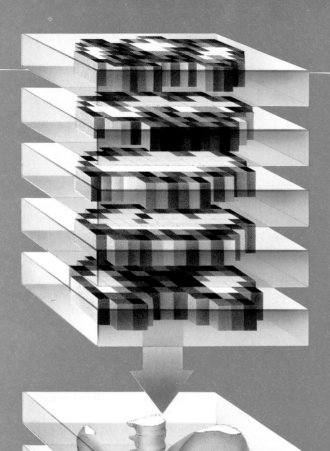

Stacking Data for an All-Round View

The process of assembling a three-dimensional view from two-dimensional slices of data shown on this page is the kind of task that computer scientists call "computationally intensive." To form an image, the computer must store the positions of thousands of voxels *(pages 48-49)* as well as meas-

Assembling slices. The two illustrations at left show how a computer creates a 3-D image from slices of data—in this case, CT scans of a pelvis. For simplicity, the thirty or more scans needed for the reconstruction are represented as five. Acting on instructions from a technician, the computer assigns color and transparency to each voxel according to density. In this example, voxels having the density of bone are made opaque and colored white; all other tissue is rendered transparent. When the computer combines the data in the slices, the result is the three-dimensional image of the pelvis shown below.

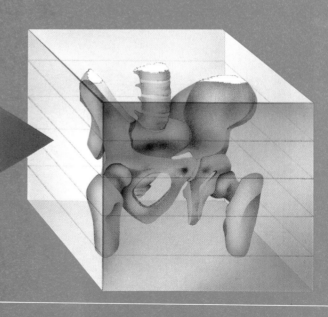

urements of the amount of x-ray energy absorbed by the tissue in each voxel during a CT scan or the radio energy emitted during an MRI scan. In addition, each voxel is assigned numbers representing color and opacity in the final image. Altogether, a typical volume rendering consists of 16 million bytes of data.

Many billions of calculations are required merely to create a three-dimensional model from this sea of information. And more work is needed to display the model as if seen from other viewpoints (below). To "rotate" the model, the computer applies a sophisticated projection technique, as if shining a light through the data into the viewer's eyes. Considering the transparency values and colors assigned to each voxel, the computer sums the attenuating effects of each voxel's opacity on the beam to render light and shadow, creating an illusion of depth.

If the voxels nearest the viewer are completely opaque, voxels deeper in the model do not appear in the image. If the nearest voxel or voxels are partially transparent, they appear as a see-through overlay.

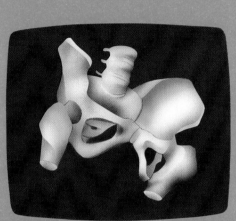

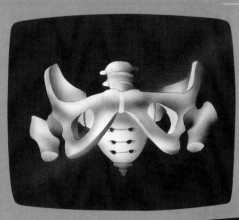

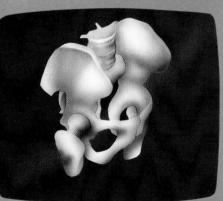

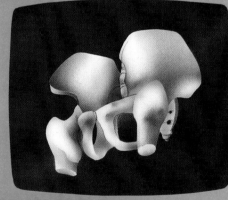

An image that spins. The figures on this page show six views of the pelvis as it would appear on a computer screen. Normally, a series of seventy-two views from different angles are captured on videotape. The images can be run sequentially to simulate a continuous rotation—or frozen for a static view.

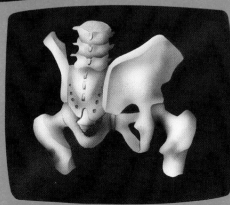

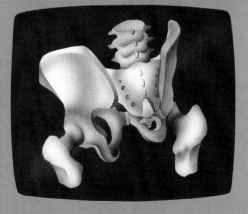

those providing funds that the idea was worth pursuing, although real effectiveness was blocked by the small number of electrodes—just eight—and the lack of precise control.

Computers had yet to enter the picture. The university's central computer had enough calculating capacity to be useful, but it was booked up for other projects and unavailable. Soon, however, the team acquired a minicomputer for their work, and development of Functional Neuromuscular Stimulation, as the technique was now called, could begin in earnest. Software was written to control more and more electrodes, providing the coordination to enable patients to stand up and walk. Such progress infused the team with optimism, even though the patients had to rely on mechanical supports, their gait was awkward, and they could remain on their feet only for a few minutes.

The minicomputer had its drawbacks. Most obviously, there was no way it could accompany its user—not even within the laboratory, which had to be festooned with cables connecting the computer in the corner to patients at the various experiment stations around the room. Portable computers introduced in the mid-1970s made the laboratory neater, but they still could not be carried about by the patients.

Enormous advances in the miniaturization of electronics have been achieved since then, however. Today's experiments are conducted with a computer the size of a paperback book that is worn in the belt and linked by cables to more than thirty electrodes, each no thicker than a human hair, implanted where nerves enter muscles.

AN AUTOMATIC WALKER
Users control the system with an eight-position joystick and four push buttons. A two-line liquid-crystal display attached to the processor presents menus for various activities—standing, sitting down, walking, stepping to the side, and climbing or descending stairs. Joystick movement selects the activity; two buttons tell the computer when to start or stop, and two others regulate the speed. A person can direct the walking cycle manually, one foot movement at a time, or put the system on automatic so that pressure sensors on the feet signal when each step is completed and the next is to begin.

The strength of a muscle contraction is regulated by the length of time each electric pulse is applied; the pulse period can range from 10 to 250 millionths of a second. The duration of muscle movement is controlled by the number of pulses. Some muscles are used two or three times during the course of making one step, and each use requires a different strength and duration of movement. Altogether, the computer issues more than 1,500 commands to thirty-two muscles during each step.

Many problems remain to be solved. The stimulated movements are still awkward and tiring. Weeks of training are needed before a patient can walk just a few hundred feet—and some are never able to learn.

NEURAL SWITCHBOARDS
At Stanford University and the Veterans's Administration Medical Center in Palo Alto, California, Morton Grosser and Joseph Rosin are pursuing a related dream—but in a very different way. These scientists hope, in time, to be able

to reactivate paralyzed muscles without any artificial assistance—no wires, no pulse generators, not even a computer. Their goal is the restoration of natural nerve connections so that the nervous system can direct movement as it does in healthy people.

Most paralysis is caused by breaks in nerves. A nerve is much like a telephone cable—a bundle of wires, each of which carries a separate signal. The ends of a severed cable must be rejoined by carefully splicing each of the wires together; if the ends are simply butted together, the signal will be transmitted haphazardly. In a nerve, those wires are called axons, and there can be as many as 2,000 of them, each about one micrometer in diameter—one one-hundredth the thickness of a human hair. Microsurgery techniques can reconnect nerves, but not individual axons, so that any function that is restored is the result of incomplete and almost accidental joining of these minuscule fibers.

Grosser and Rosen would replace surgical attachment with an ingeniously contrived silicon chip, implanted between the severed nerve endings. The chip, while functioning much like an old-fashioned telephone switchboard, would use twentieth-century semiconductor technology to complete the necessary neural connections. Passing through each chip would be as many as 2,500 holes, insulated from one another, into which the axons would be encouraged to grow from each direction. Meanwhile, a neurologist using microscopic electrical probes would locate the position in the chip of the axons that need to be connected to restore function. The connections would finally be made by using an electric current to destroy selected portions of the insulating material—a technique now used to customize inexpensive mass-produced chips.

Such a restored path for nerve signals would not be perfect, nor does it need to be, according to Grosser. Because nerve fibers transmit many duplicate signals, he thinks that even if just 20 percent of the axons are correctly linked, "we'll get 80 percent or more of original function."

THE FUTURE IS NOW

The list of proposed alliances between microelectronics and the human body is a long and exciting one. Eyeglasses containing miniature cameras and microprocessors could one day deliver vision: Surgeons and computer scientists have teamed up to implant electrodes in the brains of blind volunteers, who can be made to see rudimentary shapes in television images that are processed and transmitted to the brain by computers.

Other researchers are exploring the uses of computer technology to create speech and re-create the senses of touch and smell. The medical future may bring sensor "pills" that, once swallowed by a patient, will relay information about the body's inner workings to a physician's computer outside. Someday, tiny robot surgeons may navigate through diseased arteries to clean out clogging debris and repair damage.

In a 1970s television series titled *The Six Million Dollar Man*, fictional scientists reconstructed the body of a former astronaut who had been maimed in a plane crash. Damaged arms, legs, muscles, eyes, and ears were rebuilt, replaced, and made better than new by their futuristic medicine. Today, the price tag attached to that bionic wizardry looks far too low, but the prospects of its real-world accomplishment do not seem so far-fetched at all.

Treatment Previews in 3-D

Three-dimensional imaging techniques have proved a boon in many areas of medicine, from the reshaping of an infant's deformed skull to the planning of radiation therapy for cancer. For example, a 3-D view offers considerable assistance in repairing joints and bones that have worn out or that no longer work because of injury, arthritis, or cancer.

When orthopedic surgeons plan operations, the extra detail and dimension provided by 3-D images is invaluable advance information. A hipbone that has been ravaged by osteoarthritis, for example, can be viewed from all angles to deter-

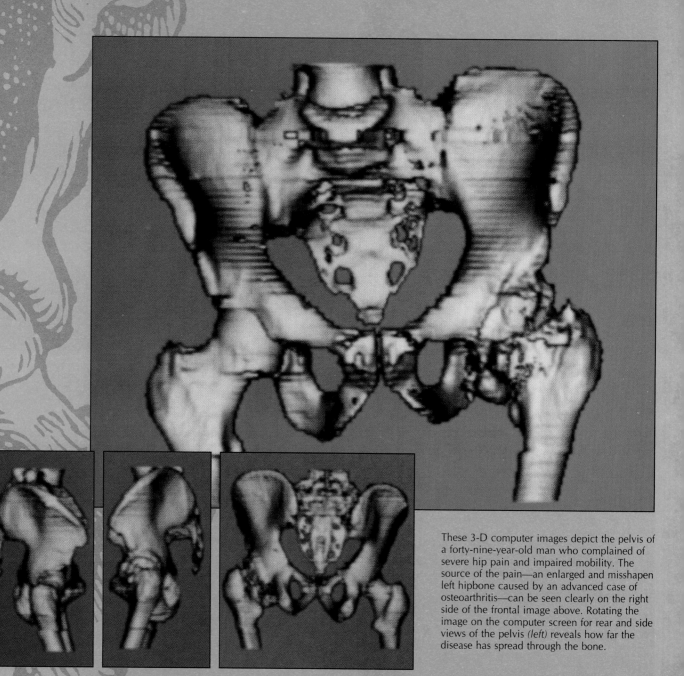

These 3-D computer images depict the pelvis of a forty-nine-year-old man who complained of severe hip pain and impaired mobility. The source of the pain—an enlarged and misshapen left hipbone caused by an advanced case of osteoarthritis—can be seen clearly on the right side of the frontal image above. Rotating the image on the computer screen for rear and side views of the pelvis *(left)* reveals how far the disease has spread through the bone.

mine whether the damage is extensive enough to require a total hip replacement.

Three-dimensional computer images are also revolutionizing the design and fitting of prostheses—artificial joints and bones. In the past, surgeons had to cut and reshape their patients' bones on the operating table in order to get most prostheses to fit. Now, with the assistance of 3-D computer graphics, custom prosthetic devices can be designed and built to fit with an accuracy of 98 percent. The age, weight, and way in which a patient moves can also be programmed into the design of the artificial joint or bone, ensuring a minimum of follow-up problems.

In the future, 3-D images may make it possible for orthopedic surgeons to try out various surgical approaches on a patient before entering the operating room. A surgeon about to operate on a patient with an abnormal gait, for example, could experiment with various changes in the alignment of the patient's knee or hip. The surgical reconfigurations that produce the most normal gait on the computer screen will then serve as a blueprint for the real thing.

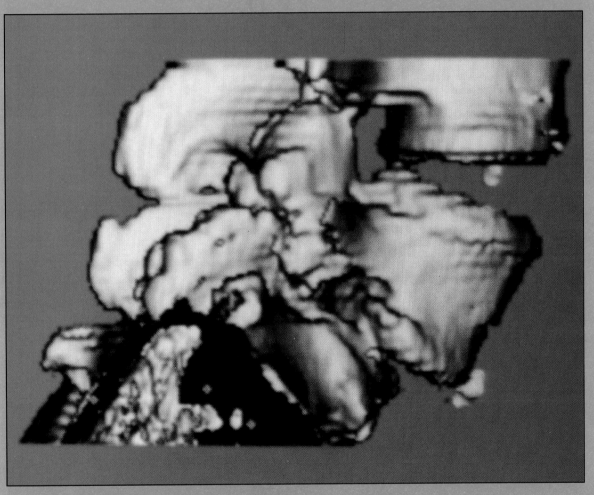

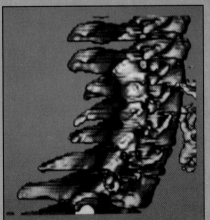

Three-dimensional images from two patients offer very different views of the spine. The image above shows a sixty-one-year-old woman's lower backbone at the point where the spine meets the sacrum, or top part of the pelvis. The squarish spine segment in the center of the picture has slipped forward, and the joint beneath it has degenerated, causing lower back pain. The spinal segments shown at left are the cervical bones, or neck, of a thirty-eight-year-old woman. Taken after an automobile accident, the image shows no abnormalities, only the normal smooth curvature of the spine.

Reshaping a Child's Skull

Three-dimensional computer graphics provide priceless reconnaissance to surgeons approaching the repair and restructuring of a deformed face or skull. Whether the deformity is the result of a traumatic injury or a congenital defect, as was the case of the young child pictured here—the ability to project a three-dimensional model of a skull onto a computer screen supplies a remarkably clear view of what the doctors can expect to find on the operating table.

The relationship between the skull bone and the surrounding soft tissue—skin, fat, and muscle—is far more evident in

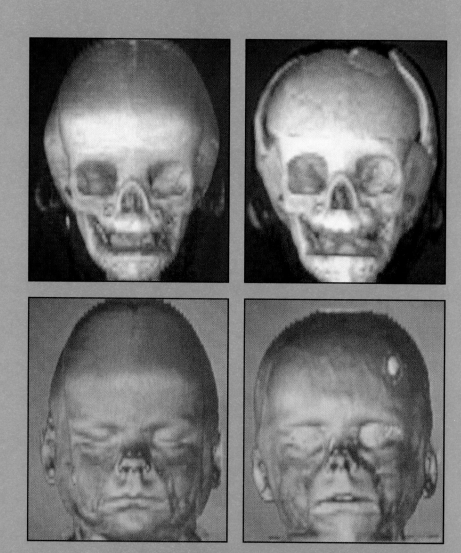

These 3-D pictures of the skull of a six-month-old baby girl were taken before and after surgery to correct a congenital abnormality of the skull known as sagittal synostosis. The condition, which does not damage the brain in any way, is the result of a premature fusing of the bone plates of the skull, causing the head to grow in an exaggerated front-to-back direction. It is corrected by removing extra bone and reshaping the skull. The upper images on both these pages show the child's skull only, while the lower images reveal an additional layer of skin and muscles. By studying the location of the muscles, nerves, and blood vessels that cover the bony skull, the surgeon was able to mold them successfully during the operation. The gaps in the skull *(upper right)* will gradually fill in with bone and close as the infant grows.

3-D images than in the flat, two-dimensional representations produced by conventional x-rays or even by CT scans. Three-dimensional images also help delineate the subtle contours of the face and can pick up subtle defects in the skull that other imaging techniques might miss.

Even more sophisticated planning tools are in development. Researchers are experimenting with 3-D computer programs that may one day help surgeons simulate the cutting and reshaping of a patient's skull; such run-throughs will make it easier to predict the outcome of a particular opera-

tion. Special programs are also being designed to enable surgeons to mirror the "good" side of an injured face onto the deformed side—again, as a kind of preoperative procedure.

Because it enables a physician to plan surgery with greater precision, 3-D imaging can mean fewer operations for people who must undergo facial or skull reconstruction. This benefits all such patients, but none more so than young children, who can have their deformities repaired before they experience the emotional scars that often result from physical abnormalities.

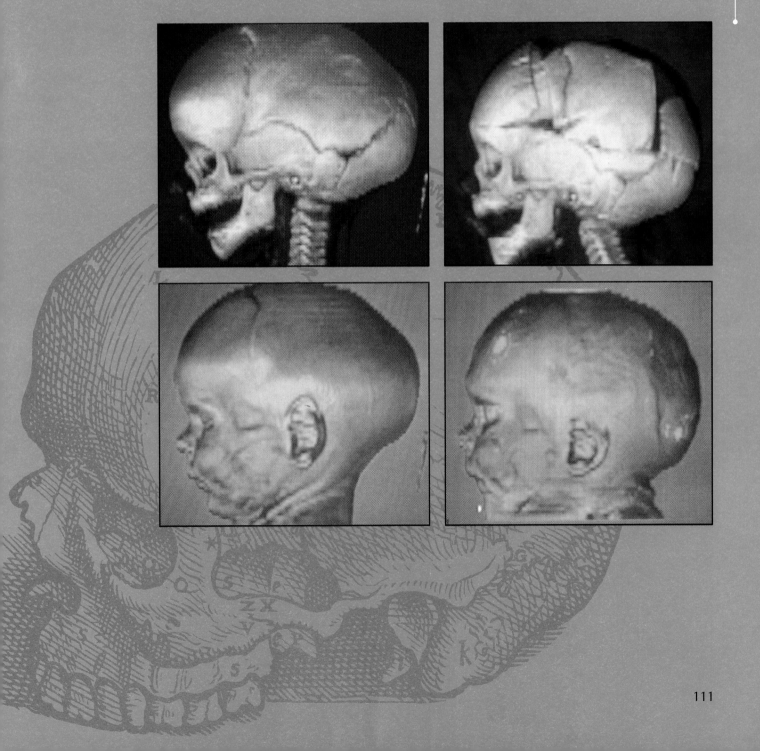

Targeting Tumors

As cancer therapists have harnessed more powerful beams of radiation to destroy tumors, pinpoint aiming has become even more important, since the beams act with equally damaging effect on healthy tissue. Three-dimensional computer graphics allows a degree of precision that was impossible with older imaging methods. With 3-D images, radiation therapists can determine not only a tumor's precise shape and location but its density as well. They can then calculate on the

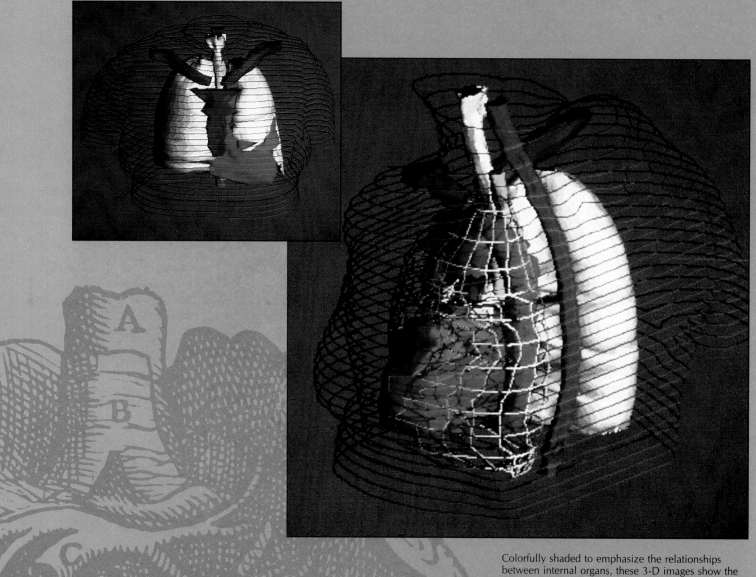

Colorfully shaded to emphasize the relationships between internal organs, these 3-D images show the chest of a woman with lung cancer. The tumor, tinted violet, is clearly visible against the white backdrop of the lungs in the smaller frontal view above. In the larger image, the angle of view has been rotated and the left lung converted into a wire frame so that the full extent of the tumor is evident and its relationship to the heart *(red)* clearly seen.

computer the exact dose of radiation that will penetrate to the target tumor but not beyond.

The placement of radiation shielding—the large lead-alloy blocks that are positioned over the patient during radiation therapy to ensure that only the tumor receives the full effect of the rays—is also made easier and more precise with 3-D imaging. Using the computer, a radiation therapist can get a beam's-eye view (below, lower right) of the radiation's path.

As a further guarantee of the beam's accuracy, lightweight molds are made of each patient at the time CT scans are taken. Later, during radiation therapy, the mold can be used to hold the patient in exactly the same position as when the planning scans were made.

Once a tumor has been identified, radiation therapists can use the 3-D images to geometrically work out how best to aim the radiation beams. In the case of the lung-cancer patient, the therapists decided to cross-fire on the tumor, a tactic that would avoid exposing healthy tissue to the full dose of radiation. The smaller image indicates where the beams intersect the outer surfaces of the patient's body.

This beam's-eye view outlines the rectangular area that will be hit by one of the radiation beams. The tumor is completely enclosed within the area. Because a small portion of the spinal cord (green) falls within the outline as well, shielding blocks will be used to protect it from the radiation.

A Visual Odyssey into the Brain

More fraught with peril than any other type of operative procedure, neurosurgery requires the utmost in dexterous skill and precision planning. Because of the brain's crucial role in the functioning of the entire body, meticulous care

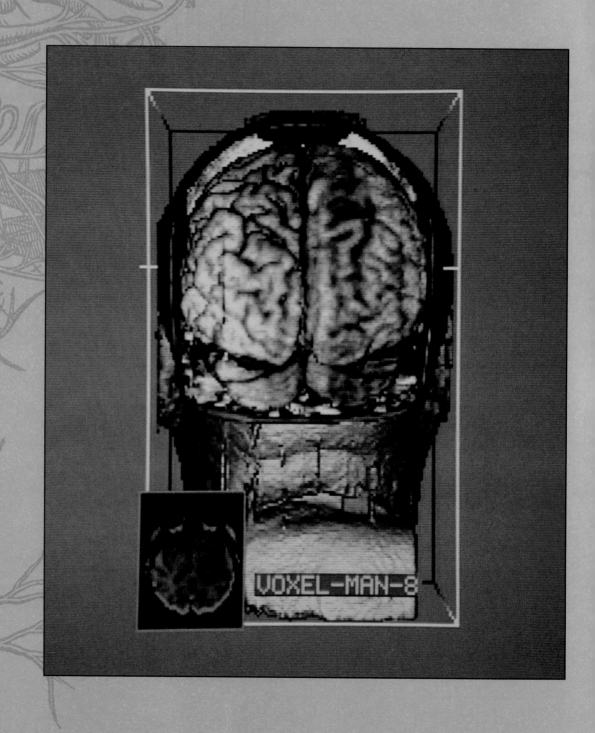

must be taken to minimize the damage to healthy tissue whenever neurosurgery is performed. In fact, some brain tumors are ruled inoperable because of the grave risks associated with reaching them: One wrong move might permanently impair some vital physical or mental capability.

As illustrated on these pages, however, state-of-the-art 3-D imaging techniques should dramatically improve the neurosurgeon's ability to chart safe courses through the human brain's intricate weave of tissues, blood vessels, and nerves. Magnetic resonance imaging (MRI) is particularly effective at noting the subtle physical distinctions between a tumor and the different types of brain tissue, thus helping a surgeon to be more precise in finding the least harmful pathways to deep-seated tumors.

In addition to visual references, some imaging programs also provide mathematical coordinates (below) that pinpoint the location of selected features. These numerical guideposts may one day be used in conjunction with computer-aided surgical instruments to bring unprecedented digital accuracy to the delicate work of operating on the brain.

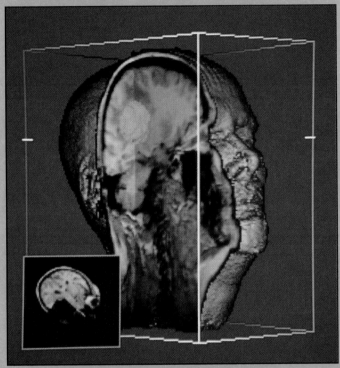

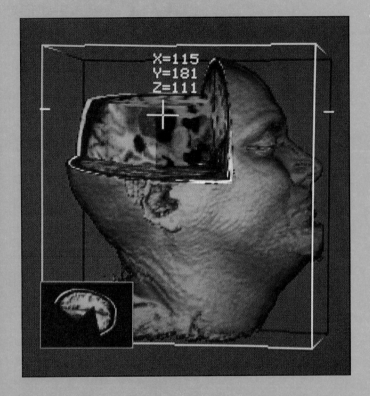

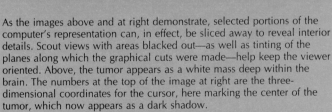

As the images above and at right demonstrate, selected portions of the computer's representation can, in effect, be sliced away to reveal interior details. Scout views with areas blacked out—as well as tinting of the planes along which the graphical cuts were made—help keep the viewer oriented. Above, the tumor appears as a white mass deep within the brain. The numbers at the top of the image at right are the three-dimensional coordinates for the cursor, here marking the center of the tumor, which now appears as a dark shadow.

◀ Reconstructed from 128 cross-sectional views taken by an MRI scanner, this 3-D image reveals the brain of a sixty-year-old woman. Slight deformation of the right hemisphere denotes the presence of an underlying tumor. The inset, known as a scout view, shows the horizontal slice that lines up with the two white tick marks on the larger image. The label VOXEL-MAN-8 identifies the program that created the image.

Glossary

Algorithm: a set of clearly defined rules and instructions for the solution of a problem. Computer programs essentially consist of the step-by-step procedures of algorithms.

Amino acid: the basic chemical constituent of proteins; the sequence of a protein's amino acids determines its structure and function.

Analog: the representation of a continuously changing physical variable (sound, for example) by another physical variable (such as electrical current).

Arthroscopy: the examination or surgical repair of the interior of a joint, such as the knee, performed by inserting a specially designed instrument called an arthroscope through a small incision.

Biopsy: the removal and examination—typically under a microscope—of living tissue for diagnostic purposes.

Bit: contraction of "binary digit," the smallest unit of information in a binary computer, represented by a single zero or one.

Brain map: a graphic depiction, usually in color, of activity taking place in the brain.

Byte: a sequence of bits, usually eight, treated as a unit for computation or storage.

CARTOS (computer-aided reconstruction by tracing of serial sections): a computer imaging system that translates two-dimensional photographs and video images of tissue slices into three-dimensional displays of features such as nerves.

Catheter: a tube that is inserted into a vessel or passageway in order to inject or withdraw fluids.

Cathode-ray tube (CRT): a television-like display device with a screen that lights up where it is struck from the inside by a beam of electrons.

Central processing unit (CPU): the part of a computer that interprets and executes instructions. It is composed of an arithmetic logic unit, a control unit, and a small amount of memory.

Chaos theory: a branch of theoretical science that attempts to determine the order underlying apparently chaotic physical systems.

Chemotherapy: the treatment of disease—typically cancer—by chemical agents.

Chip: an integrated circuit, made up of thousands of transistors and other electronic components formed on a single piece of semiconductor material.

Chromosome: one of forty-six X-shaped threads found in the nucleus of a cell and composed primarily of DNA.

Computed tomography (CT): a medical imaging technique in which x-ray beams are passed through the body from many directions in a single plane to yield an image of tissues many times clearer than an ordinary x-ray picture.

Deoxyribonucleic acid (DNA): a molecule consisting of four types of chemical bases linked in a pair of spiral strands. DNA—the primary ingredient of chromosomes—carries all the genetic information necessary for the creation of an organism and directs the production of proteins.

Digital: pertaining to the representation, manipulation, or transmission of information by discrete, or on-off, signals.

Digitize: to represent data in digital, or discrete, form or to convert an image or continuous analog signal to such a form.

Disk: a round magnetized plate, generally made of plastic or metal, used for storing data.

Electrocardiogram: a record of the electrical activity occurring in the heart as it contracts and relaxes.

Electroencephalogram: a record of the electrical activity that takes place in the brain.

Expert system: a computer program that mimics the reasoning powers of a human expert, drawing conclusions and generating advice through the manipulation of extensive data on a given subject. *See also* Inference engine; Knowledge base.

Gene: the segment of information along a DNA strand that directs production of a specific protein.

Genome: the complete genetic information contained in all forty-six chromosomes of a cell.

Hardware: the physical apparatus of a computer.

Hodgkin's disease: a cancer of the lymph system in which disease-fighting cells of the lymph nodes grow rapidly and abnormally, leaving the body vulnerable to infections.

Inference engine: the section of an expert system that comprises the procedures for manipulating data.

Interactive system: a computer system in which information and graphics are changed or manipulated in immediate response to a user's input.

Joystick: a hand-held lever that can be tilted in various directions to manipulate a computer-generated image on a display screen or to direct the movement of a computer-controlled device.

Knowledge base: the database of an expert system, consisting of the facts and inferences from which conclusions are drawn.

Knowledge engineer: a computer specialist who translates a human expert's knowledge and reasoning methods into a form that can be processed by an expert system.

Lymphoma: a group of diseases of the lymph system characterized by abnormal growth of cells in lymph tissue.

Magnetic resonance imaging (MRI): a medical imaging technique that relies on the response of hydrogen atoms to a magnetic field to distinguish between various types of soft tissue.

Memory: the internal storage facilities of a computer, as opposed to external storage devices, such as disks or tapes.

Menu: a list of the commands or functions of a particular computer program from which a user can choose.

Microcomputer: a desktop or portable computer, based on a microprocessor and intended for use by an individual; also called a personal computer.

Micrograph: a graphic representation of an object viewed under a microscope.

Microprocessor: a single chip containing all the elements of a computer's central processing unit.

Mouse: a hand-held input device that, when rolled across a flat surface, causes a cursor to move in a corresponding way on a display screen.

Neural network: an electronic circuit whose parts imitate the interaction of neurons in the brain.

Neuron: a nerve cell.

Nuclear imaging: a medical imaging technique in which a natural substance, such as glucose, is tagged with a radioactive marker and then injected into the patient; radiation emitted as the substance is absorbed by organs or tissues is detected and analyzed by a computer to produce an image. *See also* Positron emission tomography.

Nucleus: in a cell, the central spherical structure that contains all forty-six chromosomes and controls many of the activities of the cell; in an atom, the positively charged center, which consists of protons and neutrons and is surrounded by negatively charged electrons; the nuclei of hydrogen atoms contain only one proton each.

Photomultiplier tube: an instrument used to detect and amplify very low levels of light.

Photon: the smallest unit of electromagnetic energy.

Pixel: short for picture element; one of the thousands of points on a computer screen from which digital images are formed.

Positron emission tomography (PET): a form of medical imaging in which positrons, or positively charged electrons, emitted by a radioactive substance injected into the patient provide data about the workings of the brain or other organs.

Program: a sequence of detailed instructions for performing some operation or solving some problem by computer.

Prosthesis: an artificial replacement for a missing body part, such as an arm or leg.

Protocol: the experimental plan for the treatment of a disease.

Proton: one of three particle types (the neutron and the electron are the others) that make up an atom; protons carry a positive electrical charge.

Radioactivity: the spontaneous decay of an atom's nucleus, resulting in the emission of subatomic particles and radiation.

Ray sum: in computed tomography (CT) scanning, a measurement of the amount of radiation that is absorbed by bone and tissue during each exposure.

Software: instructions, or programs, that enable a computer to do useful work; contrasted with hardware, or the actual computer apparatus.

Subroutine: a self-contained section of a computer program that can be separately prepared and referred to by a single name.

Synthesizer: an electronic device for the production and control of sound; linked to a computer, a voice synthesizer translates written words into speech.

Transducer: a device that converts one form of energy to another, sound to electricity for example. Many medical sensors utilize transducers in order to convert pressure or temperature into an electric current that can be measured and recorded by computer.

Ultrasound: in medical imaging, a technique in which high-frequency sound waves are sent into the body, and their reflections, created by bodily structures and tissues, are displayed on a screen or turned into a photograph.

Voxel: short for volume element, the cube of data collected by any of several medical imaging techniques and representing the density of tissue at one specific location. An image is created by assigning colors or shades of gray to voxels in relation to their density values.

X-ray crystallography: a technique in which x-rays are used to study the molecular structure of crystallized substances, such as proteins, that are too small to be viewed under a microscope.

Bibliography

Books

Anbar, Michael, ed., *Computers in Medicine*. Rockville, Maryland: Computer Science Press, Inc., 1987.

Artificial Intelligence, by the Editors of Time-Life Books (Understanding Computers series). Alexandria, Virginia: Time-Life Books, Inc., 1986.

Bowe, Frank:
 Comeback: Six Remarkable People Who Triumphed over Disability. New York: Harper & Row, 1981.
 Handicapping America: Barriers to Disabled People. New York: Harper & Row, 1978.

Changeux, Jean-Pierre, *Neuronal Man: The Biology of Mind.* New York: Pantheon Books, 1985.

Come, Patricia Challender, ed., *Diagnostic Cardiology: Noninvasive Imaging Techniques.* Philadelphia: J. B. Lippincott Company, 1985.

Computer Images, by the Editors of Time-Life Books (Understanding Computers series). Alexandria, Virginia: Time-Life Books Inc., 1986.

Considine, Douglas M., ed., *Van Nostrand's Scientific Encyclopedia.* 6th edition. New York: Van Nostrand Reinhold Company, 1983.

De Groot, J., *Correlative Neuroanatomy of Computed Tomography and Magnetic Resonance Imaging.* Philadelphia: Lea & Febiger, 1984.

Dreyfus, Hubert L., and Stuart E. Dreyfus, *Mind over Machine: The Power of Human Intuition and Expertise in the Era of the Computer.* New York: The Free Press, 1986.

Drlica, Karl, *Understanding DNA and Gene Cloning.* New York: John Wiley & Sons, 1984.

Esser, Peter D., ed., *Digital Imaging: Clinical Advances in Nuclear Medicine.* New York: The Society of Nuclear Medicine, Inc., 1982.

Gleick, James, *Chaos: Making a New Science.* New York: Viking, 1987.

Hoffman, William, and Jerry Shields, *Doctors on the New Frontier: Breaking Through the Barriers of Modern Medicine.* New York: Macmillan Publishing Company, Inc., 1981.

Jennett, Bryan, *High Technology Medicine.* Oxford, England: Oxford University Press, 1986.

Kak, Avinash C., and Malcolm Slaney, *Principles of Computerized Tomographic Imaging.* New York: IEEE Press, 1988.

Kurzweil, Raymond, *The Age of Intelligent Machines.* Cambridge, Massachusetts: Kurzweil Computer Products, 1988.

Lehrer, Steven, *Explorers of the Body.* Garden City, New York: Doubleday & Company, 1979.

Lusted, Lee B., *Introduction to Medical Decision Making.* Springfield, Illinois: Charles C. Thomas, 1968.

McCorduck, Pamela, *The Universal Machine: Confessions of a Technological Optimist.* New York: McGraw-Hill Book Company, 1985.

Maddox, Sam, ed., *Spinal Network.* Boulder, Colorado: Sam Maddox, 1987.

Oldendorf, William, and William Oldendorf, Jr., *Basics of Magnetic Resonance Imaging.* Boston: Martinus Nijhoff Publishing, 1988.

Pagels, Heinz R., *The Dreams of Reason: The Computer and the Rise of the Sciences of Complexity.* New York: Simon and Schuster, 1988.

Panati, Charles, *Breakthroughs: Astonishing Advances in Your Lifetime in Medicine, Science, and Technology.* Boston: Houghton Mifflin Company, 1980.

Revolution in Science, by the Editors of Time-Life Books (Understanding Computers series). Alexandria, Virginia: Time-Life Books, Inc., 1987.

Rhodes, Philip, *An Outline History of Medicine.* London: Butterworths, 1985.

Shorter, Edward, *The Health Century.* New York: Doubleday, 1987.

Singer, Sam, *Human Genetics: An Introduction to the Principles of Heredity.* San Francisco: W. H. Freeman and Company, 1978.

Sprawls, Perry, Jr., *Physical Principles of Medical Imaging.* Rockville, Maryland: Aspen Publishers, Inc., 1987.

Stwertka, Eve, and Albert Stwertka, *Computers in Medicine.* New York: Franklin Watts, 1984.

Sylvester, Edward J., and Lynn C. Klotz, *The Gene Age: Genetic Engineering and the Next Industrial Revolution.* New York: Charles Scribner's Sons, 1983.

Takahashi, Shinji, ed., *Illustrated Computer Tomography: A Practical Guide to CT Interpretations.* New York: Springer-Verlag, 1983.

Thompson, Thomas T., *A Practical Approach to Modern Imaging Equipment.* Boston: Little, Brown and Company, 1985.

Periodicals

Adler, Steven J., et al., "Three-Dimensional Computed Tomography of the Foot: Optimizing the Image." *Computerized Medical Imaging and Graphics,* Vol. 12, 1988.

Albrecht, Lelia, "With Thomas Hutchinson's Marvelous ERICA, a Flick of an Eye Brings Help to the Helpless." *People,* July 20, 1987.

Allman, William F., "How the Brain Really Works Its Wonders." *U.S. News & World Report,* June 27, 1988.

Alper, Joseph, "Industry's New Magic Lantern." *High Technology,* April 1984.

Amato, Ivan, "Microtools: Small Things Considered." *The Washington Post,* March 13, 1988.

"American, Briton Share Nobel Prize for Medicine." *The Wall Street Journal,* October 12, 1979.

". . .and Cormack, Hounsfield for Medicine." *Physics Today,* December 1979.

Anderson, R. M., R. M. May, and A. R. McLean, "Possible

Demographic Consequences of AIDS in Developing Countries." *Nature,* March 17, 1988.

Argento, Joanne, "DXplain: Diagnoses at Your Fingertips." *Physicians & Computers,* March 1988.

"Artificial Intelligence Is Here: Computers That Mimic Human Reasoning Are Already at Work." *Business Week,* July 9, 1984.

"Automation for Handicapped: Control Is Key." *Computers & Medicine,* October 1987.

Barnett, G. Octo, et al., "DXplain: An Evolving Diagnostic Decision-Support System." *The Journal of the American Medical Association,* July 3, 1987.

Barrett, Charles N., "Preoperative Planning with Interactive Graphics: The Dawning of a New Era." *Computer Graphics World,* March 1984.

Bartusiak, Marcia, "Designing Drugs with Computers." *Discover,* August 1981.

Batcha, Becky, "Diagnosis with the Touch of a Finger." *Computerworld,* January 18, 1988.

Batson, Trent, "The ENFI Project: A Networked Classroom Approach to Writing Instruction." *Academic Computing,* February 1988.

Bernstein, Jeremy, "Cosmology." *The New Yorker,* June 6, 1988.

Biondetti, Pietro R., et al., "Three-Dimensional Surface Reconstruction of the Carpal Bones from CT Scans: Transaxial versus Coronal Technique." *Computerized Medical Imaging and Graphics,* Vol. 12, 1988.

Bleich, Howard L., et al., "Clinical Computing in a Teaching Hospital." *The New England Journal of Medicine,* March 21, 1985.

Bleich, Howard L., Jerome D. Jackson, and Harold A. Rosenberg, "PaperChase: A Program to Search the Medical Literature." *M.D. Computing,* Vol. 2, No. 2, 1985.

Blum, Bruce I., "Clinical Information Systems—A Review." *The Western Journal of Medicine,* December 1986.

Booth, William, "CDC Paints a Picture of HIV Infection in U.S." *Science,* January 15, 1988.

"Braille 'Mouse' Lets the Blind Use Computers." *The New York Times,* December 24, 1986.

Brody, Jane E., "Lasker Award Winners Include Two Working on X-Rays of Brain." *The New York Times,* November 13, 1975.

Brown, Hannah, "Hello, Mr. Chips." *New York Post,* March 15, 1988.

Brownstein, Mark, "Drivers Vocalize Screen Displays: Screen Talker Designed to Aid Sightless Users." *InfoWorld,* February 15, 1988.

Burrough, Bryan, "Second Chances: A Wave of Communications Devices Brings a Renewed Sense of Hope to the Handicapped." *The Wall Street Journal,* November 10, 1986.

"Can Computer Model Focus AIDS Control?" *Computers & Medicine,* November 1986.

Cannon, Gordon, "Sequence Analysis on Microcomputers." *Science,* October 2, 1987.

Carey, Joseph, "How Medical Sleuths Track Killer Diseases." *U.S. News & World Report,* October 14, 1985.

Caruso, Denise, "Micros Break Silence for Deaf Editor." *InfoWorld,* March 19, 1984.

Castillo-Chavez, Carlos, Daniel Grunbaum, and S. A. Levin, "Designing Computer Models of the Spread of HIV (Human Immunodeficiency Virus)." *Forefronts,* September 1987.

Chase, Marilyn, "Voice-Activated Robot to Aid Quadriplegics Is Research Aim." *The Wall Street Journal,* August 29, 1986.

"Computer: Key to AIDS Cure." *Computers & Medicine,* July 1986.

"Computer for Baby Reduces Disability Lag." *Computers & Medicine,* July 1988.

Connell, C., et al., "Automated DNA Sequence Analysis." *BioTechniques,* May-June 1987.

Cook, Joan, "Putting Mentally Ill in Computer Jobs." *The New York Times,* September 14, 1987.

Cosco, Joseph, "TV Paralysis Victim Will See Eye-to-Eye." *Norfolk Virginia Pilot,* October 23, 1986.

Cunha, Carlos, "Take a Letter, Computer." New Bedford, Massachusetts *Standard-Times,* March 15, 1987.

Dean, Andrew G., "EPIAID." *BYTE,* October 1985.

DeJean, David, "Hope & Glory: Men, Medicine, & PCs." *PC/Computing,* September 1988.

Denning, Peter J., "The Science of Computing: Computer Models of AIDS Epidemiology." *American Scientist,* July-August 1987.

Di Chiro, Giovanni, and Rodney A. Brooks, "The 1979 Nobel Prize in Physiology or Medicine." *Science,* November 1979.

"Does Your Computer Know How Sick You Are?" *Newsweek,* July 13, 1987.

Doherty, Richard, "Portable Reader Guides Blind." *Electronic Engineering Times,* July 18, 1988.

Donovan, Joe:
"Disabled Boatbuilder Uses Voice Technology to Tell His Story." *Caliper,* October 1987.
"Voice-Controlled Robot-Servant: A New Aide for Severely Disabled People." *American Rehabilitation,* July-August-September 1987.

Doolittle, Russell F., "Proteins." *Scientific American,* October 1985.

Dworetzky, Tom, "Opening New Frontiers in Molecular Biology." *Discover,* March 1987.

"Educated Hand Communicates for Deaf-Blind." *Computers & Medicine,* November 1987.

Elmer-DeWitt, Philip, "The Best Part Is I Can Do It All." *Time,* September 22, 1986.

Fishman, Elliot K., et al., "Three-Dimensional Imaging and Display of Musculoskeletal Anatomy." *Journal of Computer Assisted Tomography,* 1988.

"For the Blind, a Spreadsheet That Talks." *The Wall Street Journal,* February 6, 1987.

Fox, Charles, "Stephen Hawking: A Man for All Time." *PC/Computing,* August 1988.

Fries, James F., "Time-Oriented Patient Records and a Computer Databank." *The Journal of the American Medical Association,* December 18, 1972.

Garfinkel, David, "We Could Wire Up an Intelligent Artificial Pancreas." *Perspectives in Computing,* spring 1984.

Gordon, Richard, Gabor T. Herman, and Steven A. Johnson, "Image Reconstruction from Projections." *Scientific American,* October 1975.

Gore, Rick, "The Awesome Worlds within a Cell." *National Geographic,* September 1976.

Gorman, James, "My Fair Software." *Discover,* February 1985.

Gupta, Udayan, "Latest Devices Aid Severe Cases of Hearing Loss." *The Wall Street Journal,* March 23, 1988.

Harris, Daniel K., "Computer-Assisted Decision Support: A New Available Reality." *The Journal of the American Medical Association,* July 3, 1987.

Helix: The University of Virginia Medical Center Quarterly, spring 1988.

Hellerstein, David, "Plotting a Theory of the Brain." *The New York Times Magazine,* May 22, 1988.

" 'HELP' Monitors Patient Status and Hospital Pocketbook." *Hospitals,* May 1, 1984.

Herndon, Nancy, " 'A' Is for Apple . . . Able, Active, and All by Myself." *The Christian Science Monitor,* July 11, 1988.

Hirsch, David, "Drug Database—Online Key to Therapeutic Dilemma." *Healthcare Online,* April 1988.

Hixson, Joseph R., "Deposit 5 Cents for the Next Dx." *Medical Tribune,* August 25, 1988.

Hodgson, William A., and Kipton P. Lade, "Digital Technology in Hearing Instruments: Increased Flexibility for Fitters and Wearers." *The Hearing Journal,* April 1988.

Hubbard, Susan Molloy, Jane E. Henney, and Vincent T. DeVita, Jr., "A Computer Data Base for Information on Cancer Treatment." *The New England Journal of Medicine,* February 5, 1988.

"Inherited Wealth." *The Economist,* April 30, 1988.

"Integration Is Key to Hospital Computerizing." *Computers & Medicine,* June 1986.

"Interview: Leroy Hood." *OMNI,* November 1987.

"An Interview with Raymond Kurzweil." *SAINT (Special and Individual Needs Technology),* December 1987.

John, E. R., et al., "Neurometrics: Computer-Assisted Differential Diagnosis of Brain Dysfunctions." *Science,* January 8, 1988.

Johnson, Jeannette Seloover, "Technological Reports: An Expert System for Programming a Digitally Controlled Hearing Instrument." *Hearing Instruments,* Vol. 39, No. 4, 1988.

Jones, Robert Snowdon, "IBM Announces PC Wares for Disabled." *InfoWorld,* February 15, 1988.

Kinoshita, June, "Neural Darwinism." *Scientific American,* January 1988.

Kolata, Gina, "Mathematical Model Predicts AIDS Spread." *Science,* March 20, 1987.

Lant, Jeffrey:
"PaperChase: Medical Information at Your Fingertips." *Physicians & Computers,* February 1988.
"Search Me: The PaperChase Story." *CD-ROM Librarian,* May 1988.

Lavoie, Francis J., "In Offices, 'Disabled' Doesn't Mean 'Unable.' " *Modern Office Technology,* June 1988.

Levin, Simon A., and Viggo Andreasen, "Mathematical Models of Infectious Diseases." *Forefronts,* December 1986.

Levinson, Daniel, "AMA/NET Makes Comeback: The New Version Is Off to an Excellent Start." *Computer News for Physicians,* February 15, 1988.

Levinthal, Cyrus, "Molecular Model-Building by Computer." *Scientific American,* June 1966.

Levinthal, Cyrus, and Randle Ware, "Three Dimensional Reconstruction from Serial Sections." *Nature,* March 31, 1972.

Levitt, Harry:
"A Brief History of Digital Hearing Aids." *The Hearing Journal,* April 1988.
"Digital Hearing Instruments: A Brief Overview." *Hearing Instruments,* Vol. 39, No. 4, 1988.

Lewis, Ricki, "Computerizing Gene Analysis." *High Technology,* December 1986.

"Light Shed on How Hemoglobin Molecules Use Energy." *Hopkins Gazette,* February 10, 1982.

Lipkin, Martin, and James D. Hardy, "Mechanical Correlation of Data in Differential Diagnosis of Hematological Diseases." *The Journal of the American Medical Association,* January 11, 1958.

Longini, Ira M., Jr., "Predicting the Global Spread of New Infectious Agents." *American Journal of Epidemiology,* Vol. 123, No. 3, 1986.

McAuliffe, Kathleen, "Reading the Human Blueprint." *U.S. News & World Report,* December 28, 1987-January 4, 1988.

McGinn, Paul R.:
"Computer Diagnosis System Adds a New Dimension to Medicine." *American Medical News,* June 26, 1987.
"MEDICOM Offers On-Line Access to Drug Interaction Data." *American Medical News,* April 8, 1988.

Machlis, Sharon, "Disabled Find High Tech a Liberating Experience." *Middlesex News,* June 19, 1988.

Mahon, William J., "Digital Hearing Aids: Defining the New Breed." *The Hearing Journal,* April 1988.

Malarkey, Tucker, "English, the Write Way." *The Washington Post,* May 5, 1987.

Mallove, Eugene F., "Sequencing the Human Genome: Computers Take a Leading Role." *Computers in Science,* premiere, 1987.

"Mapping Nerves in the Brain." *Science Digest,* April 1981.

"The Mapping of Man." *The Economist,* February 20, 1988.

Marsolais, E. B., and Rudi Kobetic, "Functional Electrical Stimulation for Walking in Paraplegia." *The Journal of Bone and Joint Surgery,* June 1987.

Marx, Jean L., "Multiplying Genes by Leaps and Bounds." *Science,* June 1988.

Mattill, John, ed., "Chip Nerves." *Technology Review,* October 1987.

May, Robert M., and Roy M. Anderson, "Transmission Dynamics of HIV Infection." *Nature,* March 12, 1987.

"The Mechanical Heart." *Mechanical Engineering,* September 1984.

Meltzer, Rachel, "New Firms, Spun from Academic Programs, Bring Molecular Modeling to 2nd Generation." *Genetic Engineering News,* September 1984.

Menosky, Joseph A., "The Gene Machine." *Science 81,* July/August 1981.

Miller, Eric, "Digital Signal Processing in Hearing Aids: Implications and Applications." *The Hearing Journal,* April 1988.

"The Mind within the Brain." *Discover,* May 1984.

"Modeling Calamity." *Scientific American,* July 1987.

Nash, F. A., "Differential Diagnosis: An Apparatus to Assist the Logical Faculties." *The Lancet,* April 24, 1954.

Nathanson, Michael, "Using Artificial Intelligence Systems May Be Smartest Way to Trim Costs." *Modern Healthcare,* April 1984.

"New Ears for the Deaf." *High Technology Business,* December 1987.

Peterson, Ivars, "Heart Flow: Computer Simulations of Blood Flow in the Heart Aid Artificial-Valve Designers." *Science News,* September 27, 1986.

Peyton, Joy Kreeft, and Trent Batson, "Computer Networking: Making Connections between Speech and Writing." *ERIC/CLL News Bulletin,* September 1986.

Poggio, Tomaso, "Vision by Man and Machine." *Scientific American,* April 1984.

Porter, Martin, "Computers with Heart." *PC Magazine,* April 30, 1985.

Portugal, Franklin H., "Medical Imaging: The Technology of Body Art." *High Technology,* November-December 1982.

Preves, David A., "Digital Hearing Aids." *ASHA (American Speech-Language-Hearing Association),* September 1987.

Principi, Eugene G., Paul S. Peabody, and Ralph Korpman, "Better Care, Shorter Stays, Thanks to Networking." *Data Communications,* November 1986.

"Quadriplegic's High Tech, Low Cost Messaging." *Computers & Medicine,* July 1987.

Quint, Barbara, "Another Look at AMA/NET." *Database Searcher,* December 1987.

Randal, Judith E., "NMR: The Best Thing Since X-Rays?"

Technology Review, January 1988.

Reeke, George N., Jr., and Gerald M. Edelman:
"Real Brains and Artificial Intelligence." *Journal of the American Academy of Arts and Sciences,* winter 1988.
"Selective Neural Networks and Their Implications for Recognition Automata." *The International Journal of Superconductor Applications,* spring 1987.

Rennels, Glenn D., and Edward H. Shortliffe, "Advanced Computing for Medicine." *Scientific American,* October 1987.

Rensberger, Boyce, "Second Genetic Code's Logic Revealed: MIT Team's Findings May Prove Useful in Computers." *The Washington Post,* May 13, 1988.

Ripka, William, "Computers Picture the Perfect Drug." *New Scientist,* June 16, 1988.

Risen, James, "Robots Open Door for Disabled in the Office." *Los Angeles Times,* June 9, 1988.

Roberts, Leslie, "New Sequencers to Take on the Genome." *Science,* October 16, 1987.

Ross, Michael E., "Everyman's Guide to Life as a Paraplegic." *The New York Times,* April 27, 1988.

Rovner, Sandy, "When Words Fail." *The Washington Post,* November 13, 1985.

Rozen, Leah, "Talk May Be Cheap, but Ray Kurzweil Stands to Make Millions by Yakking to His Voice Computer." *People,* March 9, 1987.

Salmons, S., "The Eighth International Conference on Medical and Biological Engineering." *Bio-Medical Engineering,* October 1969.

Schaffer, W. M., and M. Kot, "Do Strange Attractors Govern Ecological Systems?" *BioScience,* June 1985.

Schmeck, Harold M., Jr., "New Test That Finds Hidden AIDS Virus Is a Sleuth with Value in Many Fields." *The New York Times,* June 21, 1988.

Schnier, W. R., "Capitalizing on the Digital Opportunity. *Audecibel,* winter 1988.

Semler, H. Eric, "What Technology Can Do for the Disabled." *The New York Times,* June 5, 1988.

"Sharing AIDS Data: Aim of Computer Net." *Computers & Medicine,* February 1988.

Shortliffe, Edward H.:
"Computer Programs to Support Clinical Decision Making." *The Journal of the American Medical Association,* July 3, 1987.
"Medical Expert Systems—Knowledge Tools for Physicians." *The Western Journal of Medicine,* December 1986.

Siberner, Joanne, "Pictures of the Heart." *Science News,* January 25, 1986.

Smith, Lloyd, and Leroy Hood, "Mapping and Sequencing the Human Genome: How to Proceed." *Bio/Technology,* September 1987.

Sontag, Sherry, "For Disabled, Computers Are Creating New Lives." *The New York Times,* August 24, 1985.

"Space Age Computing Aimed at Damaged Hearts." *Cardiovascular Research Report,* summer 1988.

Spivak, Jonathan, "Super X-Rays: A 'Glamour Machine' Is Hailed by Doctors as a Boon to Diagnosis." *The Wall Street Journal,* December 10, 1975.

Strehlo, Kevin, "Thoughts into Words." *PC/Computing,* August 1988.

Swerdloff, Alissa, "The Brain Builders." *Science Digest,* March 1982.

"Tachyarrhythmia Control—An Historical Perspective." *Meditronic News,* September 1979.

"Talking Book." *Enter,* April 1984.

"Talking Computer Aids Blind Typists." *Science Digest,* July 1981.

Tank, David W., and John J. Hopfield, "Collective Computation in Neuronlike Circuits." *Scientific American,* December 1987.

Thomas, Lewis, "Medicine's Second Revolution." *Science 84,* November 1984.

"To Deaf, 'Flat' English Needs Computer Rise." *Computers & Medicine,* May 1988.

"The Transplant Revolution." *Maclean's,* November 23, 1987.

"Triumph of the Odd Couple." *Time,* October 22, 1979.

Tucker, Jonathan B., "Designing Molecules by Computer." *High Technology,* January 1984.

Twedt, Steve, "CMU Robot May Give Disabled a Better Chance at Employment." *The Pittsburgh Press,* March 27, 1988.

Ubell, Earl:

"How Computers Are Helping Doctors Treat You Better." *Parade Magazine,* March 13, 1988.

"Walking by Electricity—First Tests." *New York Herald Tribune,* October 14, 1961.

UCSF Magazine, April 1987.

Underhill, Lisa H., and Howard L. Bleich, "Bringing the Medical Literature to Physicians: Self-Service Computerized Bibliographic Retrieval." *Western Journal of Medicine,* December 1986.

Vannier, Michael W., Jeffery L. Marsh, and Robert H. Knapp, "Three-Dimensional Reconstruction from CT Scans: Disorders of the Head." *Applied Radiology,* November 1987.

Watt, Peggy, "Computers Give Independence to the Disabled." *InfoWorld,* March 19, 1984.

Weiss, Rick:

"First Human Genome Map Completed." *Science News,* October 17, 1987.

"Improving the AIDS Test: Genetic Engineers Offer a New Approach to AIDS-Antibody Testing." *Science News,* April 2, 1988.

"When Designers Think to Include Handicapped." *The Wall Street Journal,* January 7, 1988.

White, Ray, and Jean-Marc Lalouel, "Chromosome Mapping with DNA Markers." *Scientific American,* February 1988.

Other Sources

Barnett, G. Octo, et al., "DXplain: Experience with Knowledge Acquisition and Program Evaluation." *Proceedings of SCAMC—Symposium on Computer Applications in Medical Care.* The Computer Society of the IEEE, Washington, D.C., 1987.

Bertrand, William E., "Use of Microcomputers in Health and Social Service Applications in Developing Nations." *CRC Critical Reviews in Medical Informatics,* 1987.

Birnholz, Jason, "Fetal Neurology." In *Ultrasound Annual 1984.* New York: Raven Press, 1984.

Bongaarts, John, "The Demographic Impact of AIDS in Africa." Background paper prepared for the Presidential Commission on the Human Immunodeficiency Virus Epidemic, April 1988.

Borges, Gregory, et al., "Development and Operation of a Laboratory Electrical Stimulation System for Walking in Paraplegic Subjects." Paper presented at the Rehabilitation Engineering Society of North America, June 1988.

Buford, W. L., Jr., and D. E. Thompson, "A Real Time Interactive Graphical Simulation of the Thumb." 37th ACEMB, September 17-19, 1984.

"CARTOS: Modeling Nerves in Three Dimensions." Prepared by Research Resources Information, U.S. Department of Health and Human Services, May 1981.

Crick, F. H. C., "The Structure of Hereditary Material." In *Genetics: Readings from Scientific American.* San Francisco: W. H. Freeman and Company, 1981.

Dean, Jeffrey A., et al., *Epi Info Version 3: Computer Programs for Epidemiology.* Distributed by USD, Incorporated, Stone Mountain, Georgia.

Edelman, Gerald M., "Through a Computer Darkly: Group Selection and Higher Brain Function." *Bulletin of the American Academy of Arts and Sciences,* October 1982.

Engelhardt, K. G., et al., "Robotic Vocational Workstation." The Robotics Institute, Carnegie-Mellon University, Pittsburgh, Pennsylvania, February 1, 1988.

"The Gallaudet ENFI Project: Bridging the Deaf and Hearing Worlds." Transcript from a talk given by Trent Batson at the ADAPSO luncheon, December 1, 1987.

"Guide to Resources for Persons with Disabilities." IBM National Support Center for Persons with Disabilities, Atlanta, Georgia, October 1, 1987.

Kobetic, Rudi, and E. B. Marsolais, "Control of Paraplegic Gait by Detection of Discrete Events." Paper presented June 1988 at Rehabilitation Energy Society of North America.

Kobetic, Rudi, E. B. Marsolais, and S. G. Carroll, "Stimulation Patterns for Gait in Paraplegic Subjects." Excerpt from the 40th ACEMB, Niagara Falls, New York, September 10-12, 1987.

Kropf, Noel, Irwin Sobel, and Cyrus Levinthal, "Serial Section Reconstruction Using CARTOS." In *The Microcomputer in Cell and Neurobiology Research.* New York: Elsevier Science Publishing Company, Inc., 1985.

"Kurzweil Computer Products, Inc. Background Information."
Paper from Kurzweil Computer Products, Cambridge,
Massachusetts, June 1988.

Levinthal, Cyrus, "The Formation of Three-Dimensional
Biological Structures: Computer Uses and Future Needs." In
*Computer Culture: The Scientific, Intellectual, and Social
Impact of the Computer,* Vol. 426 (reprinted from *Annals of
the New York Academy of Sciences).*

Levinthal, Cyrus, and Françoise Levinthal, "On the Pathways of
Neural Development." In *Genetics of Neurological and
Psychiatric Disorders.* New York: Raven Press, 1983.

McCormick, Bruce H., et al., eds., *Visualization in Scientific
Computing: Computer Graphics.* July 1987.

Nathwani, Bharat N., et al., "Augmenting the Multidisciplinary
Approach in Diagnostic Surgical Pathology for Utilizing
Interactive Videodisc and Computer Systems." Rough draft.
University of Southern California, July 23, 1988.

"National Library of Medicine MEDLARS: The World of
Medicine at Your Fingertips." U.S. Department of Health and
Human Services, October 1986.

Philips Medical Systems, *Principles of MR Imaging.* The
Netherlands, 1984.

Report to Congress on the Decade of the Brain: *Approaching the
21st Century: Opportunities for NIMH Neuroscience Research.*
U.S. Department of Health and Human Services, January 1988.

*Research Report: Hodgkin's Disease and the Non-Hodgkin's
Lymphomas.* National Cancer Institute, Bethesda, Maryland, no
date.

"Restoring Walking in Paralyzed People." Brochure from the
Veteran's Administration Rehabilitation Research and
Development Service, no date.

Shortliffe, Edward H., "Artificial Intelligence in Management
Decisions: ONCOCIN." Department of Medicine and
Computer Science, Stanford University School of Medicine,
Stanford, California, April 1986.

Shriver, Bruce, ed., "Diagnosis by Computer: Two Decades of
Progress." *Proceedings of the Thirteenth Hawaii International
Conference on System Sciences: Selected Papers in Medical
Information Process,* Vol. 3. University of Hawaii, 1980.

Tangorra, Joanne, "The Personal Computer as Therapist." In
Digital Deli. New York: Workman Publishing, 1984.

Vannier, Michael W., et al., "Multispectral Magnetic Resonance
Image Analysis." In *CRC Critical Reviews in Biomedical
Engineering.* Boca Raton, Florida: CRC Press, Inc., 1987.

Acknowledgments

The editors wish to thank: **In England:** Cambridge—David Mason; Hayes, Middlesex—Terry Sohl, THORN EMI Central Research Laboratories. **In Germany:** Munich—Peter Seitz, Novel GmbH; Pinneberg—Karl Heinz Höhne. **In the United States:** Arizona—Tempe: John E. Brimm, EMTEK Health Care Systems; California—Foster City: Alan Roter, Applied Biosystems, Inc.; La Jolla: Arthur J. Olson, Research Institute of Scripps Clinic; Lancaster: Walt Waltosz, Words +, Inc.; Los Angeles: Ronald F. Dorfman and Bharat N. Nathwani, University of Southern California; Mountain View: William Courtney, Acuson; Pasadena: Leroy E. Hood and Kai Wang, California Institute of Technology; San Francisco: Jeff Miller, William O'Connell, and Elias H. Botvinick, University of California; Stanford: Robert S. Engelmore, Lawrence M. Fagan, Thomas Rindfleisch, Janice Rohn, and Edward H. Shortliffe, Stanford University; Colorado—Denver: Christine L. Kennedy, Softsearch; Connecticut—New Haven: Perry Miller, Yale University; Delaware—Wilmington: William C. Ripka, E. I. DuPont Experimental Station; District of Columbia—Leonard Glassman and Janet LaFleur, Columbia Hospital for Women; Georgia—Atlanta: Andrew Dean and Consuelo Beck-Sagué, Centers for Disease Control; Illinois—Chicago: William A. Yasnoff, American Medical Association; Iowa—Iowa City: Steve M. Collins and David J. Skorton, University of Iowa; Louisiana—Carville: William L. Buford, Jr. and Loyd M. Myers, Gillis W. Long Hansen's Disease Center; Baton Rouge: David E. Thompson, Louisiana State University; Maryland—Baltimore: Elliot Fishman and Derek Ney, The Johns Hopkins Hospital; Bethesda: Richard J. Feldman, National Institutes of Health; Lawrence C. Kingsland III, National Library of Medicine; Kensington: Jane Gruenebaum; Massachusetts—Boston: Edward P. Hoffer, Massachusetts General Hospital; Michigan—Ann Arbor: Benedick A. Fraass, The University of Michigan Medical Center; Minnesota—Rochester: Hillier Baker, The Mayo Clinic; Missouri—St. Louis: Michael W. Vannier, Mallinckrodt Institute of Radiology; New Jersey—Iselin: Ted Pensiero, Siemens Medical Systems; New York—Buffalo: John W. Loosk and Robert A. Spangler, State University of New York; New York: Cyrus Levinthal, Columbia University; Einar Gall, Neurosciences Institute; North Carolina—Chapel Hill: Henry Fuchs and Stephen M. Pizer, University of North Carolina; Durham: Timothy D. Fagert and G. Allan Johnson, Duke University Medical Center; Ohio—Cleveland: Carole Kantor and E. Byron Marsolais, Case Western Reserve University and Veteran's Administration Medical Center; Rhode Island—Cranston: Dominic Valentino and Richard L. Wagner, Rhode Island Medical Center; Texas—College Station: Bruce H. McCormick, Texas A and M University; Utah—Salt Lake City: Kathleen Kingston, 3M Health Information Systems; John E. Wood, University of Utah; Washington—Kennewick: Carlton Cadwell, Cadwell Laboratories, Inc.; Wisconsin—Madison: Lloyd Smith, University of Wisconsin.

Picture Credits

The sources for the illustrations that appear in this book are listed below. Credits from left to right are separated by semicolons, from top to bottom by dashes.

Cover: Art by Sam Ward. 6: Dr. William L. Buford, Jr., and Dr. Loyd M. Myers, Gillis W. Long Hansen's Disease Center, and Dr. David E. Thompson, Louisiana State University—photo and computer graphic modeling by Arthur J. Olson, courtesy Research Institute of The Scripps Clinic, La Jolla, California © 1988—Dr. Steve M. Collins and Dr. David J. Skorton, The University of Iowa Cardiovascular Image Processing Laboratory—courtesy Medical Products Department, E. I. DuPont de Nemours and Company. 8, 9: Photo and computer graphic modeling by Arthur J. Olson, courtesy Research Institute of The Scripps Clinic, La Jolla, California © 1988. 10, 11: Courtesy Medical Products Department, E. I. DuPont de Nemours and Company. 12, 13: Dr. Steve M. Collins and Dr. David J. Skorton, The University of Iowa Cardiovascular Image Processing Laboratory. 14, 15: Dr. William L. Buford, Jr., and Dr. Loyd M. Myers, Gillis W. Long Hansen's Disease Center, and Dr. David E. Thompson, Louisiana State University (top 3)—Dr. Loyd M. Myers, Gillis W. Long Hansen's Disease Center; Dr. William L. Buford, Jr., Gillis W. Long Hansen's Disease Center. 16-20: Art by Sam Ward. 22: Dr. Harry Churgani and Dr. Michael E. Phelps, UCLA School of Medicine. 24-29: Courtesy The Neurosciences Institute, New York. 31: Courtesy Professor Eduardo Macagno, Columbia University; courtesy Columbia University. 32-35: Art by Sam Ward. 36-41: Art by Al Kettler. 42: Art by Sam Ward. 45-48: Art by Stephen R. Wagner. 49: Courtesy Siemens Medical Systems, Inc. 50: Art by Stephen R. Wagner. 51: Dr. G. A. Johnson, Duke Medical Center. 52: Art by Stephen R. Wagner. 53: Courtesy UCSF Department of Nuclear Medicine. 54: Art by Stephen R. Wagner. 55: Courtesy Acuson Corporation. 56: Art by Stephen R. Wagner. 57: Art by Stephen R. Wagner—Dr. G. A. Johnson, Duke Medical Center. 58-61: Art by Sam Ward. 62-65: Dr. G. A. Johnson, Duke Medical Center. 67-69: Art by Sam Ward. 71: Reproduced by permission of the Controller of Her Majesty's Stationary Office. Crown Copyright Reserved. 73: Novel GmbH, Munich. 74: Art by Sam Ward. 76: Dr. Dominic Valentino, University of Rhode Island and Rhode Island Psychiatric Research and Training Center. 79-81: Art by Fred Devita. 82, 83: Screens by Tina Taylor—art by Fred Devita. 84, 85: Screens by Tina Taylor; Dr. Ronald F. Dorfman, Department of Surgical Pathology, Stanford University (2); art by Fred Devita. 86, 87: Art by Fred Devita; chart by Janice Rohn, Clifford Wulfman, and Christopher Lane, Stanford University; line art by Tina Taylor. 88: Art by Sam Ward. 90: MMP, Cambridge. 92: Art by Sam Ward. 94: Kurzweil Applied Intelligence, MLS/A-Kurzweil Music Systems. 96: Art by Sam Ward. 98: Kurzweil Applied Intelligence, MLS/A-"Age of Intelligent Machines." 100: Art by Sam Ward. 103: Elliot Fishman, M.D., and Derek Ney, B.S., Johns Hopkins Hospital, Department of Radiology. 104, 105: Art by Lilli Robbins. 108-111: Courtesy Mallinckrodt Institute of Radiology. Backgrounds from *The Illustrations from the Works of Andreas Vesalius of Brussels*, Dover Publications, New York. 112, 113: Dr. Daniel McShan and Dr. Benedick Fraass, University of Michigan Department of Oncology. Background from *The Illustrations from the Works of Andreas Vesalius of Brussels*, Dover Publications, New York. 114, 115: Institute of Computer Science in Medicine, University of Hamburg, Germany, courtesy Siemens Medical Imaging Division. Background from *The Illustrations from the Works of Andreas Vesalius of Brussels*, Dover Publications, New York.

Index

Krüger, Johannes: 102
Kurzweil, Raymond: *94-95*

L

Latter Day Saints Hospital (Salt Lake City): 61
Learning: computer model of, 26, *27-29;* by reading machine, 95-96
Leeuwenhoek, Anton van: 25
Levinthal, Cyrus: 30-*31,* 32, 34-35
Llinas, Rodolfo: 33
Lou Gehrig's disease: 89-90

M

Magnetic resonance imaging (MRI): 22, 23, *56-57;* three-dimensional, 103-105, *114-115;* views, 47
Marsolais, E. Byron: 102
Mason, David: 90, 91
Massachusetts General Hospital: 74, 79
Mayo Clinic: 22
Medical information management: 59-61
Medical literature: database, 59
Medication: computer-controlled release, 101-102
Medicine and computers: 17
MEDLARS (Medical Literature Analysis and Retrieval System): 59
MEDLINE: 18, 59, 67
MemoryMate: 97
Mental illness: computer approaches, 30, 33, 75-78
Meyers, Jack: 74
Mobility, human: computer-aided, 102, 106-107
Molecular biology: 34. *See also* DNA; Proteins
MYCIN: 72

N

Nash, Firmin A.: 71
Nerve connections: computer-aided, 106-107
Neural networks: 33

Neuroscience: *See* Brain: and mind
Neurosurgery: and 3-D imaging, *114-115*

O

ONCOCIN: 18, 72-73, 74, 79, *86-87*
Orthopedics: and 3-D imaging, *108-109*

P

Pacemakers: 99-101
Pancreas: computer aid for, 101-102
Patient medical records: 59-61
PDQ: 18
Pellionisz, Andras: 33
Perceptrons: 33
Personal Reader: 95
Pixels: 63
Pople, Harry: 74
Positron emission tomography (PET): *22,* 23-24
Programmable Implantable Medication System (PIMS): 101-102
Prostheses, computer-designed: 18, 109
Proteins: *10-11, 37, 42;* modeling, 34-35

Q

QMR (Quick Medical Reference): 74
Quadriplegics: computer aids for, 91-93, *98. See also* Mobility, human

R

Radiation therapy: and 3-D imaging, *112-113*
Radon, Johann: 19
Reading machine: 93-95, 96
Robotic aid: *98*
Rogers, Carl: 75
Rosenberg, Charles: 33
Rosin, Joseph: 106-107
Rvachev, Leonid A.: 70

S

Sejnowski, Terrence: 33
Sensor pills: 107

Shortliffe, Edward: 72
Software, medical diagnostic: 18
Spectrum 32: 77-78
Speech synthesizer: 90-91; and musical synthesizer, 94
Stanford University: 79, 106
Surgery, reconstructive: and 3-D imaging, *110-111*

T

TEX: 90
Thomas, Lewis: 17
Three-dimensional views inside body: of brain, *114-115;* and cancers, *112-113;* creating, *103-105;* and orthopedic medicine, *108-109;* and reconstructive surgery, *110-111*
3M Corporation: 97
Tomography: 19-20. *See also* Computed tomography; Magnetic resonance imaging; Positron emission tomography

U

Ultrasound imaging: 23, *54-55*
University of Pennsylvania: 72
University of Southern California: 79

V

Veterans Administration: 102, 106
Vision: computer-aided, 93-96, 107
Voice synthesizers: 18
Volume rendering: *103-105*
Voxels: *48-49,* 104

W

Walking: computer-aided, 102
Warner, Homer: 61
Watson, James: 42
Weizenbaum, Joseph: 75, 76
Wilkins, Maurice: 42
Woltosz, Walt: 90
Wonder, Stevie: *94*
Word processors: for handicapped, 90-92, 93; and reading machine, 95
Words +, Inc.: 90

TIME-LIFE BOOKS

EDITOR-IN-CHIEF: Thomas H. Flaherty

Director of Editorial Resources: Elise D. Ritter-Clough
Executive Art Director: Ellen Robling
Director of Photography and Research:
John Conrad Weiser
Editorial Board: Dale M. Brown, Janet Cave,
Roberta Conlan, Robert Doyle, Laura Foreman,
Jim Hicks, Rita Thievon Mullin, Henry Woodhead
Assistant Director of Editorial Resources:
Norma E. Shaw

PRESIDENT: John D. Hall

Vice President and Director of Marketing:
Nancy K. Jones
Editorial Director: Lee Hassig
Director of Production Services: Robert N. Carr
Production Manager: Marlene Zack
Director of Technology: Eileen Bradley
Supervisor of Quality Control: James King

Editorial Operations
Production: Celia Beattie
Library: Louise D. Forstall
Computer Composition: Deborah G. Tait (Manager),
Monika D. Thayer, Janet Barnes Syring, Lillian Daniels
Interactive Media Specialist: Patti H. Cass

Time-Life Books is a division of
Time Life Incorporated

PRESIDENT AND CEO: John M. Fahey, Jr.

Correspondents: Elisabeth Kraemer-Singh (Bonn);
Christine Hinze (London); Maria Vincenza Aloisi
(Paris); Ann Natanson (Rome); Dick Berry (Tokyo).
Valuable assistance was also provided by: Elizabeth
Brown and Christina Lieberman (New York).

UNDERSTANDING COMPUTERS

SERIES DIRECTOR: Lee Hassig
Series Administrator: Loretta Britten

Editorial Staff for *The Human Body*
Designer: Robert K. Herndon
Associate Editors: Jean Crawford (pictures),
John R. Sullivan (text)
Researchers: Stephanie Lewis, Tucker Jones,
Barbara Swanke
Writer: Robert M. S. Somerville
Assistant Designer: Sue Deal-Daniels
Copy Coordinator: Elizabeth Graham
Picture Coordinator: Robert H. Wooldridge, Jr.
Editorial Assistant: Susan L. Finken

Special Contributors: William Barnhill, Maureen
McHugh, Martin Mann, Gina Maranto, Susan Perry,
Joel Shurkin, Nancy Somerville, Pamela L. Whitney
(text); Edward Dixon, Sydney Johnson, Evelyn
Prettyman, Hattie Wicks (research); Mel Ingber (index)

THE CONSULTANTS

DR. G. OCTO BARNETT, one of the developers of the medical expert system DXplain, is professor of medicine at Harvard Medical School and director of the Laboratory of Computer Science at Massachusetts General Hospital.

ERIC J. HORVITZ is a scientist with the Medical Computer Science group of the Knowledge Systems Laboratory at Stanford University. He helped develop Intellipath, a medical expert system used by pathologists in the identification of tissue samples.

ROBERT J. KAISER, a senior research fellow in the Division of Biology at California Institute of Technology, has worked extensively on the prototype design for an automatic DNA sequencer.

DR. PERRY SPRAWLS is a medical physicist and is professor of radiology at Emory University of Medicine in Atlanta. He also serves as director of the Magnetic Resonance Education Center and the Division of Radiological Sciences and Education. The author of four textbooks in the field of medical imaging, he lectures worldwide on the application of high technology to medical imaging procedures.

MICHAEL J. WALKER works for the Medical Computer Science Group at Stanford University. His research interests include medical expert systems, image analysis, and molecular biology.

Library of Congress Cataloging in Publication Data

The human body / by the editors of Time-Life Books
    p.   cm.—(Understanding computers)
Bibliography: p.
Includes index.
ISBN 0-8094-6062-9
1. Medicine—Data Processing.   2. Cognitive
psychology—Data processing.
I. Time-Life Books.   II. Series.
R858.H86 1989   610'.28'5—dc19   88-29503
                              CIP
ISBN 0-8094-6063-7 (lib. bdg.)